A GOOD LIFE

A GOOD LIFE

---

15 ESSENTIAL HABITS FOR LIVING WITH HOPE AND JOY

POPE FRANCIS

Translated from the Italian by Oonagh Stransky

New York   Nashville

Copyright © 2021 FullDay srl, Milano
Copyright © 2021 Libreria Editrice Vaticana, Città del Vaticano
Translation Copyright © 2024 Oonagh Stransky
Cover design by Jeff Miller, Faceout Studio. Cover copyright © 2024 by Hachette Book Group, Inc.

Hachette Book Group supports the right to free expression and the value of copyright. The purpose of copyright is to encourage writers and artists to produce the creative works that enrich our culture.

The scanning, uploading, and distribution of this book without permission is a theft of the author's intellectual property. If you would like permission to use material from the book (other than for review purposes), please contact permissions@hbgusa.com. Thank you for your support of the author's rights.

Worthy
Hachette Book Group
1290 Avenue of the Americas, New York, NY 10104
worthypublishing.com
twitter.com/worthypub

First published in English in Great Britain in 2024 by Hodder & Stoughton, a Hachette UK company.

First Worthy edition: February 2024

Worthy is a division of Hachette Book Group, Inc. The Worthy name and logo are registered trademarks of Hachette Book Group, Inc.

The publisher is not responsible for websites (or their content) that are not owned by the publisher.

Worthy books may be purchased in bulk for business, educational, or promotional use. For information, please contact your local bookseller or the Hachette Book Group Special Markets Department at special.markets@hbgusa.com.

Scripture quotations are taken from the *The New Jerusalem Bible*, copyright © 1974 by Darton, Longman and Todd Ltd. and Doubleday, a division of Random House Inc.

Library of Congress Control Number: 2023947884

ISBNs: 9781546007029 (hardcover), 9781546007500 (ebook)

Printed in the United States of America

LSC-C

Printing 1, 2023

Contents

Fifteen Rules for a Good Life		vii
ONE:	WE ARE ALL PRECIOUS	1
TWO:	THE BEST PART OF LIFE	13
THREE:	THE ONLY MOMENT IS NOW	25
FOUR:	DANGERS TO BE AVOIDED	35
FIVE:	HUNTING FOR TREASURES	53
SIX:	…AND IN TIMES OF GRIEF	71
SEVEN:	CULTIVATE KNOWLEDGE	85
EIGHT:	DO NOT WATCH LIFE GO BY FROM A BALCONY	103
NINE:	GET YOUR HANDS DIRTY	113
TEN:	NEVER ALONE AGAIN	125
ELEVEN:	AGAINST THE CURRENT	141
TWELVE:	YOU HAVE EYES, SO CONTEMPLATE	153
THIRTEEN:	DO NOT STOP DREAMING	173
FOURTEEN:	HOW TO UNVEIL THE MARVEL THAT ABIDES IN YOU	185

Fifteen Rules for a Good Life

1. Just think: *where God planted you,* there is hope! Always have hope.

2. Jesus gave us *a light that shines in the darkness: defend it, protect it.* That light is the greatest treasure you have been granted.

3. *Do not surrender to the night.* Always remember that the first enemy to be conquered lies not outside but within. Do not make room for bitter, obscure thoughts. This world is God's first miracle and He placed the grace of wonder in our hands. Faith and hope advance side by side.

4. *Cultivate ideals.* Live for something that goes beyond your mortality. And if, one day, you are presented with a hefty bill to pay for these ideals, do not stop carrying them in your heart. Faith attains all.

5. *Believe in the existence of lofty and beautiful truths.* Trust in God the Creator; in the way the Holy Spirit propels all things towards goodness, trust in the embrace of Christ that awaits all men and women at the end of their lives. Believe, for He awaits you. The world moves forward thanks to men and women who broke down walls, built bridges, dreamed and believed even when they were surrounded by words of derision.

6. *Never for a moment think that your struggle is pointless.* Life does not end in ruin: a seed of the absolute beats in our hearts. God does not let us down. He gave us hope in our hearts; He does not want to crush it with constant frustrations. Everything is born to flourish in an eternal Spring. Even us. God created us so we would flourish. This reminds me of the poem "The Almond Tree" by the great Greek poet Nikos Kazantzakis: "The oak tree said to the almond:/ Tell me about God./ And the almond blossomed."

7. *Wherever you are, build!* If you have fallen, get to your feet! Never stay down but rise up and allow others to help you get to your feet. If you are living your life sitting down, set out on a journey! If you are paralyzed by boredom, do good works! If you feel empty or demoralized, ask the Holy Spirit to fill that void yet again.

8. *Work for peace among people.* Do not listen to those who spread words of hatred and discord. Do not listen to those voices! As different as human beings may be, they were created to live together. If there is conflict, be patient: one day you will learn that every single person holds a fragment of truth.

9. *Love all people.* Love every single person for who they are. Respect everyone's journey, be it smooth or troubled, because everyone has their own story. Each of us has our own unique story. Every child that is born is the promise of life, which always proves to be stronger than death. Every love that grows represents the power of transformation and a pining for happiness.

10. *Above all else, dream!* Do not be afraid to dream. Dream! Dream of a world still unknown, one yet to arrive. The

strength of hope lies in the belief of a Creation that extends all the way to its definitive fulfillment, when God will be everywhere and in everyone. Men and women with great imaginations have brought scientific and technological discoveries to mankind; they have crossed oceans and walked on undiscovered lands. The men and women who have sown hope are the same who overcame slavery and brought better living conditions to all. Ponder these men and women.

11. *Take responsibility for this world and for the life of every single person in it.* Reflect on how each and every injustice against a poor person is like an open wound, one that lessens your dignity. Life does not end with you: other generations will come after us and more will follow them. Every day ask God to give you the gift of courage. Remember that Jesus conquered fear for us. He conquered fear! Even our most treacherous enemy is weak when faced with our faith.

12. When you stand in fear before one of life's hardships, *remember that you do not live for yourself alone.* You were immersed in the mystery of the Trinity through Baptism; you belong to Jesus. And if one day you are scared or if you find yourself thinking that it is impossible to stand up to the vastness of evil, remember that Jesus lives inside you. Through you, He and His meekness want to conquer all of mankind's enemies: sin, hatred, crime and violence.

13. *Always have the courage of truth.* At the same time, remember that you are not superior to anyone. Remember that! You are superior to no one. Even if you are the last

person to believe in the truth, this is no reason to spurn the company of others. Even if you live in the complete silence of a monastery, bear the suffering of every human being in your heart. You are a Christian: through prayer you reconduct all to God.

14. *If you make a mistake and fall, get to your feet.* Nothing is more human than making mistakes. But do not let your mistakes become a prison. Do not get trapped by your mistakes. The Son of God came to assist the sick, not the healthy; He came for you. And if you should err again in the future, do not be scared. Rise up again! And do you know why? Because God is your friend.

15. If you are stricken with bitterness, *believe in all the people who work in the name of goodness.* Their humility holds the seed of a new world. Spend time with people who have safeguarded their hearts as though they were children. Learn from all that is wonderful and nurture your sense of awe.

Live, love, dream, believe. And, with the grace of God, never despair.

A GOOD LIFE

ONE

WE ARE ALL PRECIOUS

YOU ARE IMPORTANT

You are truly precious to God, not insignificant. You are important to Him because He made you with His hands. This is why He tends to you and thinks of you with affection. You need to trust in God: His memory is not a "hard drive" that saves and archives all our data. His memory is a tender and compassionate heart, one that takes joy in erasing all traces of evil that inhabit us. He does not keep a tally of your shortcomings; He is always keen on helping you learn from your mistakes. This is because He loves you.

His love is neither overwhelming nor oppressive, His love does not distance, silence or stay silent, His love neither humiliates nor dominates. The love of the Lord is constant, discreet and respectful; His love is free and freeing, it both heals and elevates. The love of the Lord is more about raising up than knocking down, more about reconciling than forbidding, more interested in offering new chances as opposed to condemning, keener on the future than the past.

NO ONE IS EXCLUDED FROM EXPERIENCING JOY

The greatest danger that exists in our world, rife with consumerism, is the desolation and anguish that stem from a complacent yet covetous heart, from the feverish pursuit of frivolous pleasures and from an isolated conscience. When our inner life gets caught up in its own interests and concerns, when there is no longer room for others and no place for the poor, God's voice cannot be heard; the quiet joy of His love is no longer felt and the desire to do good fades. Even the faithful are susceptible to this very real danger. Many fall prey to it and end up feeling resentful, angry and listless. This is no way to live a dignified and fulfilling life, this is not God's will, this is not the spiritual life that flows from the heart of the risen Christ.

I invite all Christians today, wherever they may be, in whatever condition they may find themselves, to renew their personal connection to Jesus Christ or to be open to an encounter with Him, to continue seeking Him out every day, unfailingly. There is no reason why anyone should feel as though this invitation is not directed at them, because no one is excluded from experiencing the joy brought by the Lord.

A GREAT CHALLENGE

Young people are the artisans of the future. Why? Because three desires live inside them.

First, they have *the desire for beauty*. When you make music, act or paint—all of which are connected to beauty—you are searching for something you enjoy: beauty. You are beauty hunters.

Secondly, they have *the desire for goodness*. They are prophets of goodness. They like wholesomeness, they like to be good. And this goodness is contagious, it helps everyone.

And thirdly, they are *thirsty for truth*. They seek out the truth. "But Father, I already have truth!" No. This is wrong. We do not possess truth, we do not carry it with us wherever we go. We encounter truth, for truth is God. To encounter truth, we must look for it.

Carry these three desires in your hearts into the future; create the future with beauty, goodness and truth. This is the challenge ahead of you.

EVEN MY WEAKNESSES HAVE MEANING

Jesus brings new meaning to our weaknesses. He reminds us that in His eyes we are more valuable than we think. He tells us He is pleased if we share our vulnerabilities with Him. He reminds us that His mercy is not afraid of our shortcomings. Above all, He heals those weaknesses that we cannot heal on our own. And He does so with love.

What weaknesses? Let us consider them: the way we feel resentment toward those who have done us harm, which we cannot heal on our own; the way we distance ourselves from others and shut ourselves in our own worlds, which we cannot heal on our own; the way we feel sorry for ourselves and complain endlessly, which we cannot heal on our own. He is the One who can heal us with His presence, with His bread, with the Eucharist. The Eucharist is a good medicine for these weaknesses. The Bread of Life heals our inflexibility and makes us docile.

The Eucharist heals by uniting us with Jesus. It helps us

assimilate His way of life: He breaks Himself into pieces and gives of Himself to our brethren, He responds to evil with goodness. The Eucharist gives us the courage to step outside ourselves and approach others and their weaknesses with love, as God does with us. This is the logic of the Eucharist: we receive Jesus who loves us and this heals our weaknesses so that we can, in turn, show love to others and help them with their weaknesses. This goes on for our whole lives.

YOUR PRECIOUS MISSION

May you comprehend the Christian message that God wants to relay to the world through your life. Let yourself be transformed. Allow yourself to be renewed by the Spirit so that your precious mission can unfold. The Lord will make it happen despite any mistakes and missteps you may have made, provided you do not abandon the path of love and remain open to His otherworldly grace, which both cleanses and enlightens.

GOD LOVES FIRST

God surprises us. We should let ourselves be surprised by God and not assume the psychology of a computer and think we know everything. What do I mean by this? In a fraction of a second, a computer gives you all the answers—there are never any surprises.

In the challenge of love, God manifests through surprises. Let us reflect on St. Matthew. A savvy businessman, he even went against his people and collected taxes from the Jews to pay the Romans, and thereby made a lot of money. Then Jesus came along, looked at him and said, "Come, follow me." Those who were with Him were surprised. "Why is He calling this man to Him when he is nothing but a traitor, a scoundrel!" they wondered. The surprise of being loved wins over Matthew and he begins to follow Jesus. That morning, when Matthew left for work and said goodbye to his wife, he never imagined that he would return penniless, asking her to prepare a banquet for Jesus. He wanted to offer a banquet to the One who loved him first, for He had offered Matthew something that was far more important than money.

Let yourselves be surprised by God! Do not be afraid of surprises; they may rattle us, they may disturb us but they also set us on a path. A love that is true will inspire you to spend your whole life dedicated to something that might not earn you anything.

THERE IS GOODNESS (EVEN WHERE WE SEE EVIL)

Jesus says that when seeds for good grain are sown in a field, weeds also sometimes grow there. Those weeds represent everything harmful that can crop up (cf. Matt. 13:24–43). The servants go to their master and ask him where all those weeds have come from. "'An enemy did this,' he replied." (v. 28) The servants want to pull up all the weeds, but their master says no, they risk pulling up the wheat together with the weeds. They need to wait for the harvest. Only then will they be able to set aside the grain and burn the weeds. This is a story about common sense.

The intention of the servants is to eradicate immediately all that is not good, the wickedness in people. But their master is wiser and more judicious. He says they need to learn to wait, that tolerating persecutions and hostility is part of being a Christian. Evil needs to be rejected, of course, but it is important to be patient with people who are wicked. A hypocritical form of tolerance that conceals ambiguities would not be acceptable; it is important to show justice mitigated by mercy. Just as Jesus came to look for sinners as opposed to those who do good, to heal the sick before tending to the healthy, so we, His disciples, must not try and suppress the wicked but save them (cf. Matt. 9:12–13). This is patience.

The Bible presents two ways of acting and interpreting the story: on the one hand, the master sees far off into the distance; on the other hand, there is the perspective of the servants, who only see the problem. The servants care about a field that has no weeds, while the master cares about obtaining good wheat. The Lord invites us to adopt the latter's vision and to focus on getting good wheat even though it may be surrounded by weeds. People who search only for the flaws and limitations in others do not cooperate well with God, unlike those who know how to recognize goodness as it grows silently in the field of the Church, those who let it grow until it matures. Then it shall be God and He alone who will reward the good and punish the wicked.

GOD FORGIVES WITH A CARESS

Jesus forgives not with a decree but with a caress. Jesus goes beyond the law and forgives by tending to the wounds of our sins. How many of us deserve to be punished! And it would be just. But He forgives! How? His mercy does not erase sin; the forgiveness of God erases it. Mercy goes beyond.

It is like the heavens: we look at the night sky and see stars but when the sun comes out in the morning with its bright light, we do not see the stars anymore. This is the mercy of God: a great light of love and tenderness.

God forgives not with a decree but with a caress. He does not humiliate the adulterous woman. He does not say to her: What did you do? When did you do it? How did you do it? And with whom? He tells her to go forth and sin no more. God's mercy is great; He forgives with tenderness.

AIM HIGH

Do not be afraid of saintliness. It will not strip you of your energy, vitality or joy. On the contrary, you will become what the Father had in mind when He created you and you will be faithful to your deepest self.

Do not be afraid to set your sights even higher: allow yourself to be loved and liberated by God. Do not be afraid to let yourself be guided by the Holy Spirit. Saintliness does not make you less human; it is the encounter between your weakness and the power of God's grace. Ultimately, As Léon Bloy said about life, "the only great tragedy is not to become a saint."

HEAL ME IF YOU SO CHOOSE!

What does it mean to have great faith? A person with great faith places their history, which may be marked by wounds, before the feet of the Lord and asks Him to heal them, to give their life meaning. We all have our own histories and they are not always "clean." Often our histories include pain, misfortune, trouble and sin. What can I possibly do about my history? Should I hide it? No! We must lay our histories before the Lord and say, "Lord, heal me if you so choose!"

DISQUIET IS A SEED

When I hear that a young man or woman is worried and restless, I feel it is my duty to assist them, to give meaning to their disquiet, because it is like a seed that will later bear fruit. And right now I feel that I need to assist with the most precious thing ever: your disquiet.

GOD IS PATIENT WITH YOU

Each of us might be that servant in the parable of forgiveness who is burdened with such great debt that he will never be able to pay it off (cf. Matt. 18:21–35). When we kneel down before a priest in the confessional, we do exactly what that servant did. We say, "Lord, have patience with me." Have you ever reflected on God's patience? He has so much patience. We are well aware of our many faults and how often we fall and sin, over and over. And yet, God never tires of offering us His forgiveness each time we ask for it. His forgiveness is great and complete, assuring us that even if we recommit the same sins He will be merciful with us and will never stop loving us. Like the master in the parable, God feels compassion, a mixture of pity and love: this is how Scripture describes God's mercy. Our Father is moved to compassion whenever we repent; He sends us home with calm hearts and at peace, letting us know that He has pardoned and forgiven us. God's forgiveness knows no bounds; it goes far beyond our imagination and can reach deep into the heart of anyone who knows they have done wrong and who wants to return to Him. God looks into the heart of the person who seeks forgiveness.

NO ONE ELSE CAN GIVE THE WORLD WHAT YOU CAN

"I want to take ownership of life, to own my own life. How do I do that?" Life is a special kind of reality: we own it solely when we give it away. This is the one way we can own our lives! But you might say, "Even if I give it my very best, life will not get better." This is not true. Do you know why? Because you are unique. Because no one else can give the world what you are called on to give. Someone once asked Mother Teresa of Calcutta the same thing. "But Sister, you do so many beautiful things for the poor and dying, but what use are they in our world, really? It is so pagan, atheistic and wicked." Mother Teresa replied, "It is a drop in the ocean, but if I do not do it, no one will."

No one can give what I, a unique being, can give. No one can give the world what you are called upon to give! Each one of you is unique and—please, never forget this—precious in the eyes of God. You are precious to the Church, you are precious to me. I wish I could tell each one of you how precious you are to me. You are precious to God. How beautiful it would be if you were to go around saying these words to each other as a greeting, straight from the heart: "You are precious, you are precious..."

TWO

THE BEST PART OF LIFE

THE MOST IMPORTANT LESSON

Today, with so many kinds of media available to us, we are well informed—even over-informed. Is this a bad thing? No. It can be good and useful, but we also run the risk of information overload. We acquire so much information that sometimes we do not know what to do with it all. Young people risk turning into "museums," storing up all sorts of facts but not knowing what to do with them. We do not need young people to be museums, we need them to be wise! You might ask, "Father, how do I become wise?" This is another challenge: the challenge of love.

What is the most important subject to study at university? What is the most important subject to learn in life? To learn to love. This is the challenge that life sets before you today. Learn to love. Do not just accumulate information without knowing what to do with it. Through love, however, all that information can bear fruit.

For this to happen, Scripture proposes a serene and tranquil path that relies on the three languages: the language of the mind, the language of the heart and the language of the hands. The three of them work in harmony: what you think, what you feel and what you do. All the information you have can travel to the heart and stir it into action. And this gets done harmoniously.

THE HARMONY OF WISDOM

We—unfortunately—are "macrocephalous." Our universities teach us endless ideas and concepts. We are the heirs of liberalism, of the Enlightenment... But we have lost the harmony of the three languages: the language of the head, or thinking; the language of the heart, which is to say, feeling; the language of the hands, or doing.

To find harmony, people need to think about their feelings and act on them, feel what they are thinking and act on that, and act on what they are thinking and feeling. This is the harmony of wisdom. I do not mean to say that specialists are inharmonious. We need specialists, we really do! But only when they are rooted in human wisdom. Specialists who are disconnected from this kind of wisdom are robots.

BEYOND LA DOLCE VITA

When I traveled to Amazonia, I met many people. I was in Puerto Maldonado, in Peruvian Amazonia. I spoke with many people from a wide range of indigenous cultures. Then I had lunch with fourteen chiefs, all of whom were dressed in traditional costume, with feathers. They spoke a language rich in wisdom and intelligence—not just intelligence, but wisdom! I asked one of the men, "What do you do?" And he replied, "I am a university professor." This indigenous man wore his feathers to the lunch but went to university in "civilian" clothing. I then asked a woman what she did. "I am the Minister of Education for the region." And so on, one after the other. Then I asked a girl what she did: "I am a student of political science." This was when I realized that we have to modify the image we have of indigenous peoples, with their feathers and arrows. By listening to them, I discovered the great wisdom of these people. I also came to understand the wisdom of "living well," as they call it. "Living well" has nothing to do with the "dolce vita" or with living on easy street. No. Living well means existing in harmony with Creation. We have lost this wisdom of living well, but the original peoples of the earth hold the door open for us.

THE VALUE OF SMALL THINGS

Christian spirituality offers an alternative interpretation of the term "quality of life" and encourages a visionary and contemplative lifestyle that allows for deep enjoyment without being obsessed with consumerism. We need to adopt an ancient lesson, one that is present in different religions as well as in the Bible: the conviction that "less is more." The constantly growing desire to accumulate consumer goods is distracting to the heart and can get in the way of cherishing each and every moment. On the other hand, by being serenely present in all situations, even those that seem insignificant, we open ourselves up to even greater horizons of understanding and personal fulfillment. Christian spirituality offers personal growth through moderation, a way of enjoying life with little. It is a return to simplicity, it allows us to stop and appreciate the small things, to be grateful for the opportunities that life affords us without being overly attached to what we possess, or sad for what we do not. In so doing, we avoid falling prey to the dynamics of dominion and the meaningless accumulation of pleasures.

IN THE END, THE ONLY WEALTH IS LOVE

At the end of our lives, the truth will be revealed and the secular notion that success, power and money give meaning to life will fade. Love, all that we have been able to give, will be revealed as the only true wealth. While those other things will fall away, love will emerge. A great Father of the Church, St. John Chrysostom, once wrote: "So it is in life: when death comes and the play is over, everyone takes off their masks of wealth or poverty and leaves this world. And they will be judged only by their works. Some will be considered truly rich and others truly poor."

WANDERING IS NOT TRAVELING

Be sure you choose the right path. What does this mean? It means learn to *travel* through life, do not *wander aimlessly without a destination*. Let me ask you a question. Do you travel or wander? Our lives are not directionless; life has a goal, a goal given to us by God. He guides us, He offers us direction with His grace. It is as if He positioned inside of us a kind of software that helps us understand His divine program so that we can respond to Him freely. But, as with every kind of software, it also needs to be constantly updated. *Keep your spiritual program updated* by listening to the Lord and accepting the challenge to do as He wills. While it is sad to see someone who has not updated their software, it is devastating when it is broken and cannot be used at all.

BE THE SOVEREIGN OF YOURSELF

Do not wait to convert to the Lord. Do not keep putting off changing your life. If you know you have this flaw, stop for a moment before going to bed and examine your conscience. Take the horse by the reins; you are in charge. Tell yourself: yes, I made a mistake, I failed multiple times, I did not succeed on many occasions but tomorrow I do not want it to happen again. It is important to be aware of our own personal failures. We all have them, every day, a multitude of them. Do not be afraid but do not let them become habitual: they should not be like salt, which you use every day. No.

If I take the reins of this passion, I will be the one in charge. I will be responsible for my actions. It only takes five minutes before going to bed to learn to become a better "sovereign" of myself the following day. Start by asking: What happened today? What happened in my soul? Let us examine our conscience every day in order to convert to the Lord. We can conclude by promising ourselves that "Tomorrow I will try not to do that again." Of course, it might happen again but maybe to a lesser degree. Eventually you will be able to govern yourself and not be governed by your passions, by all the ongoing events in your life. After all, none of us know how or when our lives will end.

It only takes five minutes at the end of every day.

EVERYTHING INVOKES MERCY

Greater than any argument to the contrary, a pleading voice exists inside every single person's heart. This voice exists within all of us. It cries out spontaneously, without anyone commanding it; it wants to understand why we are here on earth, especially in moments of darkness. "Jesus, have mercy on me! Jesus have mercy on me!" This is a prayer of great beauty. But aren't these words chiseled into all of Creation? Everything pleads and begs for the mystery of mercy to be definitively fulfilled. Not only Christians pray; they share their cry of prayer with all men and women. But the horizon extends even wider: Paul says that "the whole Creation has been groaning as in the pains of childbirth" (Rom. 8:22). Often, artists are the interpreters of this silent cry of Creation that fills every being and makes itself felt in our hearts; humankind is "a beggar before God." This is a beautiful definition of humankind: "a beggar before God."

THE LOVE OF CHRIST IS NOT A SOAP OPERA

The love of which John speaks in the Gospels is not the same kind of love that you see in a soap opera! No, it is altogether different. Christian love has a unique quality: tangibility. Christian love is concrete. Even Jesus, when He speaks of love, tells us concrete things: give food to the hungry, visit the sick.

When this tangibility is lacking, people end up living a Christianity of illusions because they do not understand the centrality of the message of Jesus. When love is not concrete, it becomes an illusion. This is akin to what happened to the disciples when they saw Jesus walking on water and thought He was a ghost, as we read in Mark 6:45–52. But an illusory love, one that is not concrete, is not good for us. When does this happen? The answer is stated clearly in the Scriptures. When the disciples think they see a ghost, it is because they did not comprehend the multiplication of the loaves and their hearts had grown hard. If you have a hard heart, you cannot love. You think that love is being dreamy. No! Love is concrete!

We need one fundamental criteria to abide inside of love: faith in the incarnation of the Word, the Word of God made Man. There is no true Christianity without this fundamental belief.

This criteria has some consequences: the first is that love exists more in deeds than in words. Jesus Himself said that it is not those who talk a lot and call out to Him—"Lord, Lord!"—who will enter the kingdom of heaven, but those who do the will of God. The first criteria is to love through deeds and not with words. The wind carries away words: today they are here, tomorrow they are gone.

The second criteria for tangibility is this: in love it is more important to give than receive. The person who loves, gives. He or she gives things, life; he or she gives himself or herself to God and others. On the other hand, the person who does not love and who is selfish always tries to receive. They always try to obtain something, to take advantage. Therefore, the advice I give is to live with an open heart, not like the disciples, whose hearts had closed. Abide in God and God will abide in us. Abide in love.

GREAT CHOICES LEAD TO A GREAT LIFE

Life is a time for making robust, decisive, eternal choices. Trivial choices lead to a trivial life; great choices lead to a great life. We become what we choose, for better or for worse. If we choose to steal, we become thieves. If we choose to think only of ourselves, we become self-centered. If we choose to hate, we become angry. If we choose to spend all our time on a cell phone, we become addicted. But if we choose God, we grow in His love every day. If we choose to love others, we find true happiness. This is how things are: *the beauty of our choices depends on love*. Never forget this. Jesus knows that if we are self-absorbed and indifferent, we remain paralyzed; but if we give ourselves to others, we become free. The Lord wants us to be full of life and He tells us the secret to it: we possess life only by giving it away. This is a rule of life: we can possess life, now and in eternity, only by giving it away. Each day, our heart is filled with choices. Allow me to give you one piece of advice to help you make good choices. If we look within, we often discover two opposing questions. One asks, *What do I feel like doing?* This question is often misleading: it suggests that what really counts is thinking about ourselves and indulging in our wishes and impulses. The question that the Holy Spirit plants in our hearts is a different one: *What would be good for me to do?* This is the choice we have to make on a daily basis. Should I do what I feel like doing or should I do what would be good for me? This self-questioning can lead to either frivolous choices or decisions that go on to shape our lives; it depends on us.

THREE

THE ONLY MOMENT IS NOW

THE NEW LIFE

When Jesus entered the town of Nain in Galilee, He encountered a funeral procession for a young man, the only son of a widowed mother. As we read in Luke 7:13–14, Jesus was deeply affected by the woman's devastating grief and He miraculously brought her son back to life.

The Gospel does not mention the name of the young man whom Jesus brought back, allowing readers to identify with him. Jesus says to you, to me, to all of us, "Get up." How well we know that even we Christians stumble and fall. We also know that we must always get up again (Lk. 7:14). Only those who are not on a journey do not fall—nor do they move forward. This is why we need to welcome the presence of Jesus in our lives and put our faith in God. The first step is to let ourselves get back on our feet. The new life that Jesus will grant us will be good and worth living because it will be supported by the One who will always be by our side, helping us live this life in both a virtuous and productive manner.

It will truly be a new Creation, a new birth. It will not be a form of psychological conditioning. Perhaps, in times of difficulty, many of you have heard people say those "magic" words that are so fashionable nowadays and which supposedly resolve all our problems: "Believe in yourself," "Find your inner strength," "Use your positive energy." These phrases are mere words; they do not work for those who are "dead" inside. The Word of Christ is both more substantial and infinitely superior. It is divine and life-affirming; it alone can bring back life in places where it has been extinguished.

WE ARE IN DEBT

Long before we learned how to think, we were thought about. We were loved before we learned how to love. We were desired much before our hearts conceived of desire. If we look at life in this way, the words "thank you" become the driving force of our days. And yet, how often we forget to say "thank you." Christians, like all believers, bless God for the gift of life. To live is, above all, to have received life: we are all born because someone wanted life for us. And this is only the first in a long series of debts that we incur by living. Debts of gratitude.

More than one person has gazed on us with pure eyes, freely, during the course of our lives. These people are often educators or catechists, people who went beyond the duties of their roles. And they managed to stir gratitude within us.

When you thank someone, you communicate with certainty that they are loved. And this is a huge first step: to know that you are loved. You show that love is the force that holds up the world.

TRUE LOVE MAKES US BEAUTIFUL INSIDE

Trust in Jesus. After saying *give*, He adds, *and you shall be given*. God is your Father and He will give you far more than you can ever imagine. God never leaves you empty-handed. When it feels like He is taking something from you, it is only to make room for something else, something better, to help you advance on your path. He liberates you from the false promises of consumerism and makes you free inside. Jesus makes you happy inside—not on the outside. Jesus does not do makeovers! He brings you inner happiness, he makes you beautiful inside! Not on the outside. He gives you what no object can—not the latest smartphone, the fastest car or the trendiest outfit. Not only will those things never be enough, they will never give you the joy of feeling loved or the joy of loving. This is true joy: to feel loved and to love.

WHEN THE MAKEUP COMES OFF

Some people are Christian in appearance only: they put on the costume of a Christian but, in the moment of truth, we discover they are only wearing makeup. And we all know what happens when someone wearing makeup gets caught in the rain without an umbrella: the mask slips and true appearances are revealed.

YOUNG TREES AND STRONG ROOTS

I have occasionally admired beautiful young trees with branches that reach high, high up into the sky, trees that look like songs of great hope. I have also seen those same trees after a storm, fallen and lifeless. They had spread out their branches too widely without first putting down firm roots and, consequently, were knocked down by the force of nature. Just like those trees, it pains me to see how young people are sometimes encouraged to build a future without even having roots, as if the world were just beginning. It is impossible to grow unless we have strong roots to support us, to keep us firmly grounded. It is easy to "float away" when there is nothing to hold on to, nothing to affix yourself to.

Roots are not anchors that chain us to the past, they do not impede us from facing the present or building something new. On the contrary, they represent a stability that allows us to grow and face new challenges.

WHAT ARE MY ROOTS?

Allow me to ask you this: in these times of crisis, do you have roots? I want each one of you to ask your heart, "What are my roots?" Have you lost them? "Am I a young person with roots or am I uprooted?" Are you rooted in the culture of your people? Are you rooted in the values of your people or your family? Or do you exist in the clouds, "full of hot air," without a foundation? "But Father, where can I find roots?" you ask. You can find so many roots in your culture! You can find them in dialogue with others. You can find them, above all—and let me underline this—in talking with the elderly. Speak with the elderly, listen to them. "But Father, they always say the same thing!" Listen to them just the same. Argue with them; if you argue with the elderly, they will express themselves more deeply and will reveal a great number of things. They will provide you with roots that—in your hands—will grow into hope that will blossom in the future. Hope blossoms in many ways but always with roots. Without roots, all is lost: hope cannot be created without roots. A poet once said, "What a tree has in bloom is nourished by what lies below ground." Find roots.

THREE PIECES OF ADVICE FROM THE HOLY SPIRIT FOR A GOOD LIFE

1. **Live in the present**
   The first piece of advice offered by the Holy Spirit is: "Live in the present." Not the past or the future but the present. The Paraclete affirms *the primacy of the here and now* in the battle against the temptation of feeling paralyzed, whether it is from bitterness, from nostalgia for the past or from focusing too intently on worries and fears about the future. The Holy Spirit reminds us of the grace that is the present. There is no better time for us: here and now is a unique and unrepeatable moment when we can do good, when we can experience life as a gift. Let us live in the present!
2. **Seek out unity**
   The Paraclete advises us to "Seek out the whole." Not a part but the whole. The Spirit does not mold isolated individuals but shapes us into a Church as diverse as our gifts, into a unity that is never uniform. The Paraclete affirms *the primacy of unity*. The Spirit chooses to operate and bring about newness in wholeness, in community. Let us look at the Apostles. They were all very different. For example, there was Matthew the tax collector, who collaborated with the Romans, and then there was Simon

the zealot, who fought against the Romans. The two had opposing political ideas and different visions of the world. But after receiving the Spirit, they learned not to focus on their secular points of view but on the wholeness of God. If we listen to the Spirit today, we will not dwell on who among us is conservative or progressive, traditionalist or innovator, right-wing or left. If those are the criteria we adopt, then the Church has forgotten the Spirit. The Paraclete drives us toward unity, accord and *the harmony of diversity*. The Spirit encourages us to see ourselves as parts of the same body: brothers and sisters. Let us seek out unity! Our Enemy wants diversity to become conflict and for this reason turns it into ideology. Say "no" to ideology and "yes" to unity.

3. **Put God before self**

   The third piece of advice the Spirit gives us is: "Put God before yourself." This is a decisive step in one's spiritual life. It is not the sum of our merits and achievements but a humble openness to God. The Spirit affirms *the primacy of grace*. We can make room for the Lord only if we unburden ourselves; only by giving ourselves over to Him do we find ourselves; only by becoming poor in spirit do we become rich in the Holy Spirit. This is true for the Church, too. We save no one, not even ourselves, by our efforts alone. If we focus only on our projects, institutions and plans for reform, we will end up being concerned only about our effectiveness and efficiency, we will only grow horizontally and, consequently, will never bear fruit. We must be wary of ideologies that divide and separate. The Church is not a human institution—or rather, it is human but not solely human—it is the temple of the Holy Spirit. Jesus brought the flame of the Spirit to the earth and the

Church is reformed by the anointing of grace, the gratuity of this anointing of grace, the power of prayer, the joy of our shared mission and the disarming beauty of poverty. Let us put God first!

FOUR

DANGERS TO BE AVOIDED

THE PRINCE OF THE WORLD IS DECEPTIVE

Let us reflect on how the prince of the world tried to trick Jesus into temptation during His forty days in the desert. Jesus was fasting and he tempted Him: "Do not worry! Are you hungry? Eat. You are allowed to eat." He also sought to persuade Him by appealing to His vanity: "You came to save humanity. Stop wasting time, go up on the roof of the temple and throw yourself off so everyone will understand the miracle and all will be done: then you will become powerful." But let us stop and reflect on how Jesus never replied to the prince with words! Never. He went and asked for the Word of God and replied to the prince with that.

Just as the prince did with Jesus, so he will attempt to do with us. "Go on, do it...it's only cheating a little...There is no harm in it...It is a minor infraction," he will say, trying to lead us down a slightly crooked path.

Jesus tells us: "I am sending you out like sheep among

wolves. Therefore, be as shrewd as snakes and as innocent as doves" (Matt. 10:16). If, however, we let ourselves be tricked by vanity and think we can fight the wolves by becoming like wolves ourselves, they will eat you alive. If you stop being a sheep, you no longer have a shepherd to defend you and, consequently, you will fall prey to the wolves.

You might ask, "But Father, what weapon can I use to defend myself from this kind of seduction: the bright fireworks that the prince of the world uses and his flattery?" The weapon is the same one that Jesus uses: the Word of God, followed by humility and meekness. Consider Jesus when He is slapped. What humility He shows, what meekness. He could have insulted them and, instead, he merely asks a meek and humble question. Consider Jesus during the Passion. The prophet says that He was led "like a lamb to the slaughter ...he did not open his mouth" (Isa. 53:7). This is humility. Humility and meekness: these are the weapons that the prince of the world, the spirit of secularity, cannot handle; he offers us temporal power and wealth and appeals to our vanity. He cannot abide by humility and meekness.

THE LAZY WILL NOT ENTER THE KINGDOM OF HEAVEN

God detests laziness and loves action. Lazy people will not be allowed to inherit the voice of the Lord. Do you understand? I am not talking about doing movement to stay in shape, running every day to get exercise. No, I am not talking about that. Here I mean allowing your heart to be moved, *putting your heart into movement.*

Think of young Samuel. He spent day and night in the

temple but was in constant movement; he did not think only about business matters but was constantly searching. If you want to hear the voice of the Lord, set out on a path, live in search of it. The Lord speaks to those *who are searching*. Those who search, move forward. Searching is always healthy, but feeling as though you have already arrived at your destination, especially in young people, is tragic. Do you understand? Never feel as though you have already arrived! Never!

IF WE FORGET THE GOOD THINGS

Do we always remember to praise God? Do we thank Him for the great things He does for us? Do we thank Him for every single day that He gives us? Or for how He always shows us love and forgiveness? Or for His tenderness? Do we thank Him for having given us His Mother, or for the brothers and sisters He sets on our path, or because He opened heaven to us? Do we thank and praise God for these things? If we forget all the good He does, our hearts shrink. But if, like Mary, we remember the great things that the Lord does, if we were to praise Him at least once a day, then we would be taking a great step forward. Once a day we can say: "I give praise to the Lord." Even "Blessed be the Lord" is a short prayer of praise. This is what it means to praise God. By saying this short prayer, our hearts will expand and our joy will grow. Let us ask Our Lady, the portal to heaven, for the grace to begin each day by raising our eyes to heaven, towards God, so that we can say to Him the same way that children say to adults: "Thank you!"

THREE ENEMIES OF GOODNESS

Three enemies are always lurking at the entrance to our hearts: narcissism, victimhood and pessimism.

1. *Narcissism* leads us to idolize ourselves, to be content only when things work out in our favor. The narcissist thinks, "Life is good when I profit from it." As a result, he or she ends up wondering, "Why should I donate my time to others?" Narcissism does great ill: it leads us to think of our needs only, to be indifferent to those of others, and never to admit our own weaknesses and errors.
2. The second enemy, *victimhood*, is equally as dangerous. Self-proclaimed victims complain each day about their brethren. "No one understands me, no one helps me, no one loves me, everyone blames me!" How often we hear these complaints! The hearts of these people close up while they continue to ask, "Why don't others take care of me?" Victimhood is thinking that no one understands us or feels the way we do.
3. Third and finally, there is *pessimism*. Here the daily complaint is, "Everything is rotten: society, politics, the Church..." The pessimist is angry with the world but does not do anything about it. "Why should I volunteer or donate? What purpose does it serve, anyway? It is pointless." Pessimism does so much damage, always seeing the dark side of things, always complaining that things will never go back to the way they once were! For people who live like this, the last thing to return is hope.

By praying to these three idols—the "mirror-god," the complaint-god ("I only feel myself when I complain") and the negativity-god ("everything is dark, the future is bleak")—we bring on *a famine of hope*. In actual fact, we need to appreciate the gift of life, the gift that each one of us represents. We need the Holy Spirit, the gift of God; He removes these three idols and heals us from the wounds inflicted by the mirror, our own complaining and darkness.

INDIVIDUALISM

Individualism does not make us freer, more equal or more friendly towards each other. The mere sum of individual interests can never generate a better world for humanity. Nor can it save us from the many ills that are continuously spreading across our globe. Radical individualism is the most difficult virus to crush. It is deceptive and leads us to believe that we should give free rein to our ambitions, as if pursuing our ambitions and forging our own safety nets somehow serves the common good.

THERE IS A PLAGUE WORSE THAN COVID

When we see a brother or sister make a mistake or if we notice they have a weakness of character, the first thing we usually do is go and tell others about it; we gossip. Gossipers shut the door of the heart on community, gossipers shut the door that leads to the unity of the Church. The greatest gossiper is the devil, who always says bad things about others. He is a liar; his goal is to break down the Church, to separate brothers and sisters and to disintegrate community. Please, brothers and sisters, let us try not to gossip. Gossip is a plague worse than Covid! Let us make all efforts not to gossip. Our brother or sister who made a mistake needs silence and prayer, never gossip.

DO NOT JUDGE OTHERS

Kindness in the community, like giving up your spot for someone else, is a virtue that has been somewhat forgotten over time. There are so many enemies of kindness, starting with gossiping, or the way people enjoy saying bad things about others, boxing their ears a little. It is a common practice and happens daily, even to me.

These practices are the temptations of an evil spirit that does not want the Holy Spirit to bring peace or kindness to the Christian community. If we go to the parish hall, we hear the catechism ladies talking badly about the charity ladies... Such disputes always exist. Even in our families and neighborhoods. Even among friends. This is not the new life. When the Holy Spirit comes to us, we begin a new life and we become kinder, more charitable.

Do not judge others: the only judge is the Lord. If, with the grace of God, we manage never to gossip, we will have made much progress. And this will be good for all.

THE TEMPTATION OF "IF ONLY..."

Too often, when we reflect on our lives, we see only the things we lack and complain about them. And so we yield to the temptation of "If only...If only I had that job, if only I had that house, if only I had money and success, if only I did not have this or that problem, if only I was surrounded by better people! But the illusion of "if only" prevents us from seeing the good that surrounds us and from recognizing the talents we have. You might not have *that* but you have *this*, and by reverting to "If only" you forget what you have. And yet God gave us those talents, or, as they are referred to in the parable in Matthew 25:14–30, the "bags of gold." He knows us and what we are capable of. He trusts us, despite our weaknesses. God even trusts the servant who will ultimately hide his bag of gold: despite the servant's fears, He hopes that the man will use what he has received. In short, the Lord asks us to use the present moment and wait productively for His return, without nostalgia for the past. Because there's also a bad kind of nostalgia, a kind that is ugly and that can poison our soul, it makes us always think of the past and about what others are doing, never of our own hands, of the opportunities for work that the Lord gives us, of our own situations, and our own poverty.

DO YOU WANT TO BRING YOUR HATRED WITH YOU INTO THE COFFIN?

How much suffering, how many wounds, how many wars could be avoided if our lives were built around forgiveness and mercy! Even in families. How many broken families do not know how to forgive each other, how many brothers and sisters carry around resentment? Merciful love should be a part of all our relationships, whether it is between spouses, parents and children, in communities, in the Church or in society and politics.

Today, this morning, while I was celebrating Mass, I had to stop for a moment during the First Reading from the book of Sirach. The line was, "Remember the end of your life and cease from enmity" (Sir. 28:6, RSV). What a beautiful line! Remember the end of your life! Remember that you will be in a coffin; will you bring enmity with you? Think of your end and cease from feeling enmity! Leave behind all bitterness. Let us reflect on this deeply moving line. "Remember the end of your life and cease from enmity."

It is not easy to forgive. In moments of calm we say, "Yes, that person did so many bad things to me but I, too, have done many bad things. Better to forgive so as to be forgiven." But then, resentment returns. It goes away and comes back, it always comes back. Forgiveness is not something short-lived, it is a continuous action against that persistent hatred. Let us remember our end and cease with enmity.

A VACCINE AGAINST THE EPIDEMIC OF INDIFFERENCE

Compassion is our best vaccine against the epidemic of indifference. "It has nothing to do with me," "It is not my business," "It does not regard me," "It is their problem": these are phrases that indicate indifference. There is a beautiful photograph that hangs in the Office of Papal Charities. It shows an older woman coming out of a fancy restaurant on a winter night; she is dressed in a fur coat and wearing a hat and gloves and so well-protected from the cold, after eating a good meal—it is not a sin to eat well!—and standing nearby in a doorway is another woman on crutches, poorly dressed, and clearly cold... She is a homeless person, and she holds out her hand. The woman in the fur coat looks away. The photograph is called "Indifference." As soon as I saw it, I telephoned the photographer and complimented him on capturing that moment. Then I asked that the photograph be hung in the Office of Papal Charities. It is a reminder not to fall into indifference. Meanwhile, there are people who feel their compassion shifting from feelings of "I do not care about you" to "You are important to me," or at the very least to "My heart feels for you." Compassion is not just a good sentiment. It is not a pietism. It has to do with forging a new bond with others. It means accepting their burden, like the Good Samaritan who, *moved by compassion*, takes care of the wounded man that he does not even know (cf. Luke 10:33–34). The world needs this creative and active form of charity. It has nothing to do with sitting in front of a screen and commenting on others. It is about people who are willing to get their hands dirty to remove degradation and restore dignity. Having compassion is choosing not to have any enemies and seeing *a neighbor* in everyone. Having compassion is a choice.

GETTING BY

Allow me to recall the words of the Blessed Pier Giorgio Frassati, who wrote them when he was young: "Live! Don't just get by!" he said. "Live!"

Surely you understand what I mean when I say how awful it is to see young people who are "blocked." They are alive but they live—and forgive me for saying this—like vegetables. They do things, but their lives do not move forward: they remain still. It makes my heart terribly sad to see young people who are ready to retire at the age of twenty! They got old too fast...

THE TEMPTATION TO PROCRASTINATE

How frequently we put off doing things in our everyday lives! It happens so very often. And it is true even in our spiritual life! For example, we say, "I know it would be good for me to pray but today I simply do not have time…" Or else we say, "I know it is important to help others, and I will, but tomorrow." Always tomorrow. We constantly postpone things. Mary, meanwhile, invites us not to postpone things. She would like us to simply reply "Yes" to all our questions. For example, "Do I really have to pray? Yes, I do." And so I pray. "Do I have to help others? Yes, I do. How do I do that? I will find a way." I do not postpone it. While every "Yes" will cost us something, it will always cost less to us than what her courageous "Yes" cost Mary, which she offered up without hesitation when she said, "May your word to me be fulfilled," and brought us salvation (Luke 1:38).

SPIRITUAL LAZINESS

Let us be wary of spiritual laziness. Let us not say to ourselves: we are doing fine, we have our prayers and liturgies and that is enough. No! Prayer does not mean avoiding the difficulties of life; the light of faith is not just a beautiful, spiritual feeling to be experienced. No, this is not the message of Jesus. We are called on to experience an encounter with Christ so that we, illuminated by His light, can shine it all around us. We need to switch on small lights in everybody's hearts; we need to be small lanterns of the Scripture that proclaim love and hope. This is what it means to be a Christian. This is our mission.

DANGERS TO BE AVOIDED

DO YOU WANT TO LEAVE YOUR IMPRINT ON LIFE OR JUST ON THE SOFA?

There is, in life, a dangerous kind of paralysis that is difficult to identify. It takes a lot out of us to admit it. I like to describe it as "paralysis of the sofa." We often think that in order to be happy all we need is a good sofa. A sofa that is deep and comfortable, that surrounds and protects us. The kind of sofa they make nowadays, with a built-in massager that promises us hours of comfort so we can escape into the world of video games or chat online. A sofa that protects us from pain and fear, that lets us stay home without needing to go to work or to worry. This "sofa-happiness" might well be the most harmful and insidious form of paralysis that exists, and it causes young people the greatest harm of all. "What do you mean, Father?" you ask. I mean that little by little, without even realizing it, we start to get sleepy, we grow glassy-eyed and dull. Clearly, many people would prefer that our young people be glassy-eyed and dull rather than alert and eager to get involved in trying to answer God's dream and to follow the aspirations in their hearts. I ask all of you: do you want to be sleepy, glassy-eyed and dull? Do you want others to decide your future for you? Or do you want to be free, alert and ready to fight for your futures?

The truth is that we did not come into this world to "vegetate" or take it easy, to transform life into a comfortable sofa. Quite the contrary. We came into this world to leave our mark. It is a very sad thing to pass through life without leaving a mark. But when we choose the easy way, when we confuse happiness with consumerism, we end up paying a high price indeed. We lose our freedom. That is the price we are forced to pay. There are many people out there who do not want young people to be free; many people do not want good things for the young; many people would prefer them to be sleepy and dull—but free, no! We must fight this! We must defend our freedom!

JUSTIFYING YOURSELF

Some Christians insist on taking a different path: they justify their actions by pointing out their strengths, they worship human potential by stressing their own capabilities, leading to a self-centered and elitist complacency, bereft of true love. We see this in a range of attitudes which might at first seem disconnected: an obsession with the law; a desire to flaunt social and political achievements; a punctilious concern for the liturgy, doctrine and power of the Church; an exaggerated interest in pragmatism; and an excessive penchant for self-help groups and for building up oneself through sharing. Some Christians spend all their time and energy on these things, rather than letting themselves be led by the Spirit down the path of love, rather than being passionate about communicating the beauty and joy of the Word to those who have lost their way, to the vast crowds that thirst for Christ.

THE NEGATIVE SIDE OF ROUTINES

Habits seduce us by telling us there is no point in trying to change things, that we can do nothing, that things have always been this way, and that despite it all we have managed to move forward. Habits impede us from standing up to evil, we allow "things to get worked out on their own," or as others would have them. May the Lord come and wake us up, rouse us from our torpor, free us from our inertia. Let us rethink our habits, let us open wide our eyes and ears—and above all our hearts—and let ourselves be moved by what is happening around us and by the call of the Word of the Risen Lord.

THE RISK OF GIVING IN

"But we do not belong to those who shrink back," says the author of the Letter to the Hebrews (Heb. 10:39). Let me repeat that: "We do not belong to those who shrink back." This is the advice the author gives us. We are not shocked because Jesus Himself was not shocked when He saw that His joyful preaching of salvation to the poor was not well or purely received, that people shouted at Him and threatened Him, that people refused to hear His word and tried to reduce it to a form of anti-clericalism.

We are not shocked because Jesus was not shocked by having to heal the sick and by setting prisoners free amid moralistic, legalistic and clerical debates and squabbles that arose every time He did some good.

We are not shocked because Jesus was not shocked by having to give sight to the blind amid people who shut their eyes in order not to see, or who looked the other way.

We are not shocked because Jesus was not shocked that His proclamation of the year of the Lord's grace—a year that embraces all of history—provoked a public scandal in matters that in our world would barely make page three of a provincial newspaper.

We are not shocked by the fact that the preaching of the Gospel is effective; this is not because of our eloquence, but because of the power of the Cross (cf. 1 Cor. 1:17).

WHEN SLEEPING IS DANGEROUS

It is not easy to stay awake and keep vigil. Actually, it is very difficult, especially at night when sleep comes to us naturally. Jesus' disciples could not stay awake, even though He had told them to keep vigil "in the evening, or at midnight, or when the cock crows, or at dawn" (cf. Mark 13:35). They did not keep vigil during those hours: that evening, during the Last Supper, they betrayed Jesus; during the night, they dozed off; at cock crow they betrayed Him; at dawn they let Him be condemned to death. They did not stay awake. They dozed off. The same torpor can also fall over us.

1. **The slumber of mediocrity**

    There is a dangerous kind of slumber: *the slumber of mediocrity*. It comes when we forget our supreme love and move forward with indifference, concerned only with living a quiet life. But without making an effort to love God daily and awaiting the newness He constantly brings, we become mediocre, lukewarm, materialistic. This slowly eats away at our faith, for faith is the very opposite of mediocrity: it is an ardent desire for God, it is the boldness to want to change, it is the courage to show love, it is constantly moving forward. Faith is not like water that puts out flames, it is a fire that burns; it is not a tranquilizer for people under stress, it is a love story for people in love! This is why Jesus detests things that are lukewarm most of all (cf. Rev. 3:16). God clearly disdains the lukewarm.

How can we rouse ourselves from this slumber of mediocrity? With *the vigilance of prayer*. Praying is like lighting a candle in the dark of night. Prayer rouses us from our lukewarm, horizontal existence and makes us look up on high; it allows us to be attuned to the Lord. Prayer allows God to be close to us, thereby freeing us from solitude and giving us hope. Prayer oxygenates life: just as we cannot live without breathing, so we cannot live as Christians without praying. We desperately need other Christians who are willing to keep vigil over those who are slumbering; we need worshippers and mediators who are willing to bring the darkness of history before Jesus, the light of the world. We need worshippers. We have lost something of our sense of adoration, of standing in silent adoration before the Lord. This leads to mediocrity: this is what it means to be lukewarm.

2. **The slumber of indifference**

There is a second kind of inner slumber: *the slumber of indifference*. Those who are indifferent see everything in exactly the same way, as if it were night; they do not care about those around them. When everything revolves around us and our needs, when we are indifferent to the needs of others, night falls in our hearts. Our hearts grow dark. We immediately begin to complain about everything, we start to feel like victims, we end up thinking that everyone is conspiring against us. Complaints, victimhood, conspiracies. It is a vicious circle. This kind of night seems to have fallen over many people today; people call out for themselves and yet are blind to the needs of others.

How do we rouse ourselves from the slumber of indifference? With *the vigilance of charity*. To awaken us from the slumber of mediocrity, we have the vigilance of prayer. To rouse us from the slumber of indifference, there is the vigilance of charity. Charity is the beating heart of a Christian: just as a person cannot live without a heartbeat, so we cannot be Christians without doing charity. Some people even think that being compassionate, helping and serving others is for losers! Actually, it is the only gesture of triumph because it focuses on the future, on the day of the Lord, when all else will fall away and love alone remains. It is by doing works of mercy that we draw close to the Lord.

FIVE

HUNTING FOR TREASURES

AN INQUISITIVE AND CREATIVE HEART

Life these days can seem mediocre and dull. This may be because people have stopped searching for what is truly important. We are satisfied with attractive but fleeting things; glittering lights turn out to be illusions, ultimately leaving us in the dark. The light of the kingdom is not some kind of firework display, it is light. Fireworks are brief while the light of the kingdom stays with us our whole life.

The kingdom of heaven is the opposite of the superfluousness of the earthly world, the opposite of a dull life. It is a treasure that makes life new each and every day, leading it to expand toward ever broader horizons. Indeed, those who have discovered this treasure have inquisitive and creative hearts; they do not do things by rote, but invent, carve out and take new paths that lead us to love God, others and to truly love ourselves. The identifying characteristic of those who walk this path of the kingdom, those who are constantly seeking, is creativity. Creativity is the quality that takes life and gives it back to us over and over. Creative people constantly look for new ways to give life.

Jesus, both hidden treasure and pearl of enormous value, is a steady source of joy, of all the joy in the world. He is the joy of discovering meaning in one's life, the joy of feeling committed to the adventure of holiness.

FIND TIME FOR OTHERS

How important it is to teach our hearts to cherish the people and things that surround us! Everything begins with cherishing others, the world and Creation. What good is it to know so many people and things if we do not cherish them?

We should try harder to *find time for others*. Time is a treasure that we all possess and yet guard jealously—we want to keep it for ourselves. Let us ask for the grace to find time for God and our neighbor, for those who are alone and suffering, for those who need someone to listen to them and show them concern. If we find time to give, we will be amazed by the joy it will bring.

LIVING IN HOPE

Attracted by elements related to our personal interests—every single day we have new experiences—and distracted by vanity, we risk losing sight of what is essential. That is why the Lord tells everyone repeatedly: "What I say to you, I say to everyone: 'Watch!' " (Mark 13:37). Keep vigil, be watchful.

But if we have to keep vigil, it means that it is night. And indeed it is. We are not living in daylight; we are waiting for dawn, we exist in a space that is flanked by darkness and fatigue. One of these days we shall be reunited with the Lord. That day shall come, let us not lose heart. The dark night will end, the Lord shall rise, He who died on the cross for us will be our judge. Keeping vigil, staying alert and attentive means waiting for this moment and not letting ourselves be overcome by discouragement. This is what it means to *live in hope*. In the same way that before we were born our loved ones waited expectantly for our arrival, now love incarnate waits for us. And if heaven awaits us, why should we get caught up with earthly concerns? Why should we get worked up about money, fame and success, all of which are passing? Why should we waste time complaining about the night when the light of day awaits us? Why should we always be worried about making "contacts" with people who can help us advance in our careers? All these things pass. Be vigilant, says the Lord.

NEW THINGS

Hope is audacious! Brothers and sisters, let us not be afraid. Let us learn how to dream big! Let us seek out the ideals of justice and social love that are born of hope. Let us not rebuild the past—especially that which was unjust and already ill. The past is past, new things await us. The Lord promised us: "I am making everything new!" (Rev. 21:5). Let us encourage each other to dream big and search out these ideals. Let us build a future where local and global dimensions enrich each other—with each of us contributing elements of our culture, philosophy, way of thinking—so that the beauty and wealth of minor groups, even marginalized ones, can flourish. Beauty lies within them, too.

FRIENDSHIP

Friendship is a gift of life and a grace from God. Through our friends, the Lord cleanses us and leads us to maturity. At the same time, our faithful friends, those who stand by our side in times of hardship, are also a reflection of the Lord's love, they are His gentle and consoling presence in our lives. Having friends teaches us to be open, to understand and care for others, to step out of our comfort zones and isolation and share life with others. For this reason, "there is nothing so precious as a faithful friend" (Sir. 6:15, RSV).

Friendship is not a fleeting or temporary relationship but one that is stable, firm and faithful; it matures with the passing of time. Friendship is a relationship of deep affection that brings us together and, at the same time, the generosity of its love leads us to seek out good things for our friends. Even if we have differences, we always share something with our friends: an intimacy that we live with both trust and openness.

Friendship is so important that Jesus presents Himself as a friend: "I no longer call you servants... Instead, I have called you friends" (John 15:15).

FORGIVENESS AND MEMORY

Forgiving does not imply forgetting. Or rather, let us say that something that cannot be denied, minimalized or concealed can still be forgiven. Something that should never be tolerated, justified or excused can still be forgiven. Something that we should never forget—for any reason whatsoever—can still be forgiven. Forgiving freely and sincerely is a gesture of greatness that reflects God's own infinite ability to forgive. If forgiveness is done gratuitously, we can also forgive those who resist repentance and who are unable to ask to be forgiven.

Those who truly forgive do not exactly forget but they stop being dominated by the destructive force that once caused them so much suffering. They break the vicious circle and halt the advancing force of destruction. They stop injecting the spirit of revenge into society, which sooner or later will circle back and take its toll on them. In fact, revenge never truly expunges a victim's unhappiness. Some crimes are so cruel and horrendous that making the perpetrator suffer does not compensate for the misdeed; at times not even killing the criminal or torturing them by any means imaginable can be commensurate with the suffering the victim experienced. Revenge resolves nothing.

This, however, does not signify impunity. We seek an adequate measure of justice out of love for justice itself, out of respect for the victims, so that we can prevent further crimes from happening, and to protect the common good—not as an outlet for personal wrath. Forgiveness allows us to pursue justice without falling into the vicious cycle of revenge and without succumbing to the injustice of forgetting.

A FREE PERSON REFLECTS ON THEIR ACTIONS

Freedom means being able to reflect on our actions, assess what is good and what is bad, and determine what kind of conduct leads to growth. Freedom means always choosing goodness. We are free because of goodness. In this, never be afraid to go against the current, even if it is not easy! Being free and always choosing to do good is a commitment, one that will transform you into a strong individual, someone who knows how to face life, a courageous and patient person.

LIBERTY, EQUALITY, FELLOWSHIP

Fraternity stems not just from a climate of respect for individual freedoms, nor from an arena of carefully regulated equality. While these conditions serve to make fraternity possible, they do not guarantee its existence. Fraternity brings something extra to bear on freedom and equality. What happens when fraternity is not consciously cultivated? What happens when there is no political desire for fraternity? What happens when people are not educated in the name of fraternity, dialogue, mutual esteem and enrichment? Freedom gets restricted and in some ways transformed into a condition of solitude; people are free only to belong to someone or something, or to possess and exploit. This has little to do with the richness of freedom, which is oriented toward love in particular.

Equality, too, is not achieved by making abstract claims like "all men and women are equal." Those who only know how to be members of clubs create closed worlds. What place is there in those worlds for someone who is not a member but who longs to build a better life for themselves and their families?

CARRY GRATITUDE

Let us not overlook the importance of thanking people: if we carry gratitude out into the world, the world will become a better place. Maybe just a little…but that is all we really need in order to transmit hope. The world needs hope. Gratitude—the disposition toward thanking someone—transmits hope. Everything is united, everything is connected and everyone can do their part, wherever they may be.

KINDNESS

Kindness frees us from the cruelty that at times poisons human relationships, from the anxiety that prevents us from thinking about others, from the frantic flurry of activity that forgets that others also have the right to be happy. Nowadays it is hard to find the time or energy to stop and be kind to others, to say "Excuse me," "Pardon me" and "Thank you." And yet every now and then, the miracle of a kind person appears: someone willing to set everything aside to show their interest, to give the gift of a smile, to speak a word of encouragement, to take the time to listen despite the general indifference that surrounds us. If we make an effort on a daily basis to do this, we can create a healthy social atmosphere that overcomes misunderstandings and prevents conflict. The practice of being kind is not a secondary detail, nor is it a superficial, bourgeois virtue. Precisely because it is based on esteem and respect for others, once the culture of kindness puts down roots in society, it can transform lifestyles, relationships and the way that ideas are debated and discussed. Kindness facilitates consensus; it opens new pathways. Hostility and conflict, meanwhile, burn bridges.

CHASTITY

I do not want to be a moralist but I would like to use a word that is not much liked, an unpopular word. Yes, sometimes even the pope has to go out on a limb to speak the truth. Love exists in charitable works and in the way we communicate, but love is always respectful of people, it does not use people. In other words, *love is chaste*. And in this hedonistic world, in this world where pleasure and having a good time and living the good life get so much publicity, I say: be chaste. Be chaste!

All of us have experienced moments when this virtue is difficult to follow, but this is the path of genuine love, the kind that gives life, that does not use the other for one's pleasure. This kind of love considers the life of the other sacred: "I respect you, I do not want to use you." It is difficult. We all know how difficult it is to overcome an "easy" and hedonistic concept of love. Forgive me for saying something that you might not have expected to hear but, please: try and experience love chastely.

HOW IS MY HUMILITY?

Humility is the path that leads towards heaven. The word "humility" comes from the Latin word *humus*, which means "earth." Paradoxically, to arrive on high, up to heaven, we need to stay low, like the earth! Jesus teaches that "those who humble themselves will be exalted" (Luke 14:11). God does not exalt us for our gifts, our wealth or our skills but for our humility. God adores humility. God raises up those who humble themselves, who serve others. Mary, for example, gives herself no other "title" than servant; she is "the Lord's servant" (Luke 1:38). She says nothing else about herself and seeks nothing else for herself.

Today let us ask ourselves, each one of us in our heart: How is my humility? Am I trying to stand out and be recognized by others, to affirm myself and be praised? Or am I focused on serving? Do I know how to listen, like Mary did? Or do I always want to be the one to speak and receive attention? Do I know how to be discreet, like Mary was? Or am I always gossiping? Do I know how to take a step back, resolve conflicts and arguments? Or do I always try and stand out? Let us ask ourselves these questions. How is my humility?

EVEN SHAME IS A VIRTUE

We experience shame when we speak the truth: I did this, I thought that. Shame is a truly Christian virtue and deeply human. The capability of experiencing shame is a virtue of the humble. In Argentina those who do not feel any shame are called *sinverguenza*. A shameless person is someone who cannot feel shame. Instead, humility and meekness frame the life of a true Christian.

Jesus is waiting for us so He can forgive us. But going to confession should not feel like going to a torture session—not at all! It is a way of praising God: I, the sinner, have been saved by Him. Is He waiting for me so He can clobber me? No. He is waiting with tenderness to forgive me. And what if I do the same thing again tomorrow? Then I will go to confession again. Go as many times as you need. He is always there, He is waiting for us.

TRUTH SHOULD BE SAFEGUARDED

Safeguarding the truth does not mean defending ideas or becoming guardians of a system of doctrines and dogmas. It means remaining tied to Christ and devoted to the Word of God. Truth, in the words of John the Apostle, is Christ Himself, the revelation of our Father's love. Jesus prays that His disciples, although they live in the world, will not follow the criteria of this world. He prays that they will not be enticed by idols but uphold their friendship with Him. He prays that they will not bend the Scripture to human and secular ways of thinking but uphold its message in integrity. Upholding the truth means being a prophet in everyday situations, to be consecrated to the Bible and to bear witness to it even when that means going against the current. At times, we Christians seek a compromise, but the Bible asks us to be steadfast in the truth and for the truth. It asks us to offer up our lives for others. Where there is war, violence and hatred, it takes commitment to be loyal to the Scripture and to be peacemakers; our social and political choices may endanger our own lives. Only in this way can things actually change. The Lord has no use for those who are lukewarm. He wants us to be consecrated to the truth and beauty of the Scripture, so that we can testify to the joy of God's kingdom, even in the darkest night of grief, even when evil seems to have the upper hand.

PATIENCE

What is patience? It is not simply tolerating challenges or showing grim determination in the face of hardship. Patience is not a sign of weakness; it is the strength of spirit that allows us to "carry the burden," to endure, to bear the weight of personal problems and problems in our community, to accept others as different from ourselves, to persevere and do good even when all seems lost. It keeps us on the path even when we are overcome by tedium and laziness.

A UNIFIED LIFE

Sisters and brothers, if you want proof that God has touched your life, check and see if you bend down to bind the wounds of others. Today is the day to ask yourself: "As a person who has often received God's peaceful mercy, am I merciful with others? As someone who has often been fed the body of Jesus, do I make efforts to relieve the hunger of the poor?" Let us not remain indifferent. Let us not live our faith halfway, receiving but not giving, accepting the gift but not giving it. We have been granted mercy; now let us be merciful. For if love is only about us, faith dries up and becomes barren. Without others, our faith becomes disembodied. Faith dies without action (cf. Jas. 2:17). Sisters and brothers, let us be renewed by peace, forgiveness and the wounds of merciful Jesus. Let us ask for the grace to become *witnesses of mercy*. Only in this way will our faith thrive. And life will be unified.

IN PRAISE OF MODERATION

Moderation, when lived freely and consciously, is liberating. It is not a lesser existence or a less intense life. On the contrary, those who live life to the fullest and who enjoy every moment are those who have given up pecking here and there, constantly looking for what they do not have. They understand what it means to appreciate everyone and everything; they know how to feel at one with the simplest things and enjoy them. In so doing, they reduce their yearnings and diminish their fatigue and anxiety. A person can live well on little, especially if he or she makes room for other pleasures: friendly encounters, good deeds, developing musical and artistic talents, being in contact with nature, and prayer. Happiness means knowing how to limit certain needs that might daze us, thereby leaving us open to greater possibilities of life.

THE MARVEL OF HUMANITY

If someone possesses a surplus of water but chooses to save it for the sake of humanity, it is because they have attained a moral elevation that allows them to go beyond themselves and the group to which they belong. This is the marvel of being human!

HUNTING FOR TREASURES

DO NOT DEPRIVE YOURSELF OF A HAPPY DAY

Generally speaking, Christian joy has a sense of humor. We see this clearly in the writings of St. Thomas More, St. Vincent de Paul and St. Philip Neri. Lacking a sense of humor is not a sign of holiness. "Banish anxiety from your heart" we read in Ecclesiastes 11:10. We receive so much from the Lord "for our enjoyment" that, to some degree, sadness is a sign of ingratitude; we get so caught up in ourselves that we cannot see the gifts of God (1 Tim. 6:17).

With fatherly love, God says: "My son, treat yourself well...Do not deprive yourself of a happy day" (Sir. 14:11–14, RSV). He wants us to be positive, grateful and less complicated. "When times are good, be happy...God created mankind upright, but they have gone in search of many schemes" (Sir. 7:14, 29). In all situations, we should strive to be flexible, emulating St. Paul: "I have learned to be content whatever the circumstances" (Phil. 4:11). St. Francis of Assisi lived by this: he could be moved with gratitude when presented with a piece of stale bread; he joyfully praised God simply for a breeze on his face.

I am not referring here to individualistic and consumerist pleasures that abound in certain cultures today. Consumerism makes the heart heavy; while it may offer occasional, passing pleasures it does not offer joy. The joy I refer to is the kind that is shared with others: as Jesus said in Acts 20:35, "it is more blessed to give than receive" or as we read in 2 Corinthians 9:7, "God loves a cheerful giver." Congenial love increases our potential for joy because it allows us to feel joy for others: "Rejoice with those who rejoice" (Rom. 12:15). And "We are glad whenever we are weak but you are strong" (2 Cor. 13:9). On the other hand, when we focus primarily on our own needs, we condemn ourselves to a joyless existence.

CHARITY ABOVE ALL

People have the potential to develop certain habits that might look like moral values: inner strength, moderation, industriousness and others. But in order for acts stemming from these moral virtues to be well directed, it is important to understand to what degree they foster openness and union with others. This dynamism is the sense of charity that comes from God. Without it, we only appear virtuous; appearances alone can never build a shared life.

The spiritual stature of a person's life is measured by love, which, in the final analysis, is the single most important criteria for deciding the worth, or lack thereof, of a human life.

Trying to describe the experience of loving, which God made possible for us through His grace, St. Thomas Aquinas explained it as a movement that focuses on the other, with "the beloved somehow united to ourselves." Our kind attention to others makes us desire all good things for them. All this begins with a sense of esteem, an appreciation of the other. Ultimately, this is the idea behind the word "charity." Those who are loved are *caro* or dear to us, which is like saying that I place great value in them. Love implies something more than just a series of benevolent actions. These actions derive from a sense of connection to the other; we consider them precious, worthy, pleasing and beautiful (not in a physical or moral sense). Our love for that person, for who they are, inspires us to seek out the best for them. Only by cultivating this way of relating to each other shall we be able to make friendship a social experience that excludes no one and is accessible to all.

JOY IS CONTAGIOUS

St. Thomas said *"bonum est diffusivum sui"*—the Latin is not too difficult to understand!—goodness tends to spread. So does joy... Joy, true joy, is contagious, infectious. It inspires us to move forward. On the other hand, when you meet a seminarian or novice who is overly serious and sad, you think: something is not right here! The joy of the Lord is missing. The joy that led you to serve, the joy of the encounter with Jesus, which inspired you to go out and meet others and proclaim the name of Jesus is missing! There is no holiness in sadness. St. Teresa once said, "A saint who is sad is a sad saint." What good are they to us? When you see a seminarian, a priest, a sister or a novice with a long, gloomy face—like a soaking-wet blanket, one of those heavy wool ones—something is wrong! Sisters and Fathers, please! No grim faces!

FEEL SMALL TO BECOME GREAT

Recognizing one's insignificance is the starting point for growth. If we think about it carefully, we do not grow thanks to our successes and possessions but on the basis of our struggles and moments of great fragility. We mature in moments of need; that is when we open our hearts to God, to others and to the meaning of life. Let us open our eyes to others. Let us open our eyes to the true meaning of life. When we feel small in the face of a large problem, before a cross we have to bear, when faced with an illness, when we experience fatigue and loneliness, let us not be discouraged. When this happens, the mask of superficiality falls away and our core fragility starts to emerge. This fragility is what unites us, it is our common ground, our shared treasure. For God, frailties are not obstacles but opportunities.

GET UP AND BECOME WHO YOU ARE!

In today's world we are "connected" but we do not communicate. An indiscriminate use of electronic devices can keep us constantly glued to a screen. With this message, I would like to call for a cultural change centered on the words that Jesus spoke to the deceased son of the widow of Nain. In a culture that prefers to see our young people isolated and withdrawn into virtual worlds, let us instead share the words of Jesus: "Get up!" These words are an invitation to open ourselves to a reality that is much vaster than virtual. They are not a rejection of technology, which should be used as a means rather than an end. "Get up!" means many other things, too. It means: dream, take a chance, fight to change the world, rekindle your hopes and aspirations, contemplate the heavens, the stars and the world around you. Get up and become who you are!

SIX

...AND IN TIMES OF GRIEF?

WHEN WE ARE IN THE EYE OF THE STORM

The boat in which the disciples travel across the lake is beset by wind and waves; the disciples are afraid they will sink. Jesus is with them but He is sleeping in the stern. The disciples are filled with fear and cry out, "Teacher, don't you care if we drown?" (Mark 4:38).

We, too, cry out to the Lord when we are beset by the trials of life. "How can you stay there in silence and not do anything to help me?" we ask. This usually occurs when we feel like we are sinking, when love or a project we cared about is on the verge of falling apart, when we are at the mercy of unrelenting waves of anxiety, when we feel we are drowning in problems or lost on the open ocean of life, rudderless, with no safe harbor in sight. Or else when we no longer have the strength to move forward, when we are out of work, when an unexpected diagnosis makes us fear for our health or that of a loved one. There are many moments when we feel we are caught in a storm, when we feel we are close to the end.

In these situations, as in many others, we feel as though we cannot breathe for fear. Like the disciples, we risk losing sight of the most important thing. In fact, even if He is sleeping, Jesus is on the boat, *Jesus is there*. He is partaking in everything that is going on. The same exact thing happens in our lives, too. "Lord, help us!" we say, and our prayer becomes a cry for help.

Today let us ask ourselves: What winds are creating a storm in my life? What kind of waves are hindering my journey, putting my spiritual life, my family life and even my psychological life in danger? This is the origin of faith: when we recognize that we are not capable of staying afloat on our own, that we need Jesus just like sailors need stars to navigate. Faith begins when we believe we cannot survive on our own, when we realize *we need God*. When we overcome the temptation to close ourselves off, He can work wonders in us. This is the gentle and extraordinary power of prayer—and it works miracles.

NO ONE IS IMMUNE TO SUFFERING

All of us need consolation. No one is immune to suffering, pain and misunderstanding. How much pain a single spiteful remark born of envy, jealousy or anger can cause! What great suffering is caused by betrayal, violence and abandonment. What grief we experience when a loved one dies! And yet, when we live through these dramatic moments, God is never far from our sides. A few reassuring words, an understanding hug, a loving caress, a fortifying prayer: God shows His closeness to us through the consolation provided by our brothers and sisters.

THERE'S NO COMING BACK FROM THE TOMB...BUT JESUS CAME BACK!

On the night before Easter we gained a fundamental right that will never be taken away from us: *the right to hope*. It is a new and living hope and it comes from God. It is not simply optimism; it is not a pat on the back or a passing word of encouragement, uttered with an empty smile. No! It is a gift from heaven and we never could have acquired it on our own. During the pandemic, we often and tenaciously said, "Everything will be all right"; we turned to the beauty of what it means to be human and allowed words of encouragement to rise up in our hearts. But as the days passed and fears continued to grow, even the boldest hopes began to fade. The hope of Jesus is different. He plants the conviction in our hearts that God will make everything all right; He brings forth life even from beyond the grave.

Generally, no one who enters the grave ever leaves it. But Jesus did; He rose up for us, He brought life where there was death, a boulder had been placed over the entrance and He pushed it aside to start a new story. Just as He pushed aside the rock that sealed the entrance of the tomb, so He can remove the rubble that seals our hearts. Let us not give up, let us not put a stone on top of hope. We can and must hope, because God is faithful. He did not abandon us, He visited us: He came to us in situations of pain, anguish and death. His light illuminated the darkness of the tomb. Today He wants that light to penetrate even the darkest corners of our lives. Sisters and brothers, even if you have buried hope deep in your hearts, do not give up: God is great. Darkness and death do not have the final word. Be strong! God conquers all!

EVEN THE POPE GOES THROUGH HARD TIMES

Once, at a dark time in my life, I asked the Lord for the grace to free me from a difficult and complex situation. It was a dark time. I had to preach spiritual exercises to some Sisters and, on the last day, as was customary back then, they all had to confess. A very elderly Sister came to confession; she had a clear gaze, her eyes were full of light, she was a woman of God. I felt the need to ask her to pray for me and so I said: "Sister, as your penance, pray for me because I need grace. Ask the Lord for it. If you ask the Lord on my behalf, surely He will grant it to me." She was silent for a moment as if she were praying and then she looked at me and said, "Of course the Lord will give you that grace, but make no mistake: He will do it in His own divine way." What good it did to hear that the Lord always gives us what we ask and that He does it in His own divine way. His way involves the cross: not to make us suffer, but for love, love until the very end.

THOSE WHO DO NOT KNOW HOW TO CRY ARE NOT GOOD CHRISTIANS

The hardest question we ask ourselves is: Why do children have to suffer? Why? It is when our hearts manage to ask

...AND IN TIMES OF GRIEF?

this question and weep that we begin to understand. Temporal compassion is completely useless! That kind of compassion has us, at the very most, reaching into our pockets and extracting a few coins. If Christ had had that kind of compassion, He would have cured three or four people and then returned to the Heavenly Father. It was when Christ wept—and how He wept!—that He understood our troubles.

The world today needs us to weep! The marginalized weep, the neglected weep, the scorned weep, but those of us who lead a relatively comfortable life do not know how to weep. There are truths we can see only with eyes that have been cleansed by tears. I ask each one of you to ask yourselves: Do I know how to weep? Do I weep when I see a child that is hungry? Do I weep when I see a child on drugs living on the street? Or a homeless, abandoned and mistreated child? Or a child who has been exploited and enslaved by society? Or do I only know how to weep like a selfish person who cries for something that they want? This is the first thing I would like to say to you: let us learn how to weep.

In the Bible, Jesus wept. He wept for His friend who had died. He wept in His heart for the family who had lost their daughter. He wept in His heart when He saw the poor widow accompanying her son to the cemetery. He was moved and wept in His heart when He saw how the crowds resembled sheep without a shepherd. If you do not learn how to weep, you are not good Christians. This is your challenge. Be brave —do not be afraid to cry!

CONFIDE, EVEN IN TEARS

The second Beatitude says: "Blessed are those who mourn, for they shall be comforted" (Matt. 5:4). These words might seem contradictory because weeping is not typically considered a blessing, a sign of joy and happiness. Weeping and mourning are usually tied to death, illness, moral adversity, sin and mistakes. In other words, the basic, delicate and difficult issues of everyday life. We often live with wounds and are tested by ingratitude and misunderstanding. Jesus proclaims as holy those people who weep for real situations, people who, despite it all, trust in the Lord and seek comfort under His wing. These people are not indifferent, nor do their hearts grow hard with the suffering they witness. They continue to hope patiently for God's comfort. And they do not have to wait to feel this comfort; they experience it in their everyday life.

HIGHS AND LOWS, LIGHT AND SHADOW

We know well that life is made up of highs and lows, light and shadow. All of us live through moments of disappointment, failure, confusion. The Covid pandemic in particular caused us to live lives full of worry, fear and unease; then, it was easy to fall into the trap of pessimism and apathy. How should we react when faced with such emotions? Psalm 33 gives us a clue: "We wait in hope for the Lord: He is our help and shield. In him our hearts rejoice, for we trust in His holy name" (Ps. 33:20–21). In other words, a soul that waits confidently for the Lord finds comfort and courage in the darkest moments of our lives. Where does this courage and certainty come from? They are born of hope. And hope, that virtue that leads us toward our encounter with the Lord, never lets us down.

God is present throughout humanity, He is the "God with us." God is not distant, He is always with us, He often knocks on the door to our hearts. God walks alongside us in support. The Lord does not abandon us; He accompanies us through the events of our lives and helps us discover the purpose of our path, the meaning of everyday life, He gives us courage when we are under duress or suffering. In the middle of the tempest of life, God reaches out to us and frees us from dangerous situations. How beautiful this is! In Deuteronomy 4:7 the prophet says to the people: "Think of this, what other nation is so great as to have their gods near them the way the Lord our God is near us when we pray to him?" No other nation is like this. Only we have this grace of having God close by. We await God and hope that He shows Himself to us; but He also hopes that we show ourselves to Him!

EVEN FAILURES ARE GOOD

Some people live superficially, just getting by. They think they are alive while in fact they are dead within (cf. Rev. 3:1). People spiral downward even at the tender age of twenty, losing their self-worth and dignity. They follow the dictum of "let me live the way I want" and seek out instant gratification: a little fun, some crumbs of attention and affection from others... Then there is the growing digital narcissism that affects both young people and adults alike. So many people live this way! Some have embraced materialism, concerned only with making so much money they will never have to worry about it again, as if that is the goal of life. In the long run, this will inevitably lead to deep unhappiness, apathy, ennui and growing despair.

Negative attitudes can also be the result of personal failure: when something we cared about, something we were committed to, falls short of our expectations or no longer gives the desired results. This can happen in academia or in the world of sports or the arts... The end of a "dream" can make us feel dead inside. But failures are part of life and can sometimes be a grace! Frequently, something we thought would bring us happiness proves to be merely an illusion, a false idol. Idols demand everything from us and enslave us but give us nothing in return. In the end they collapse, leaving us with dust and smoke. If failure causes our idols to crumble, then it is good, even though it may lead to suffering.

KNOWING HOW TO CRY WITH OTHERS

"Blessed are those who mourn, for they shall be comforted" we read in Matthew 5:4. The world around us, however, says the exact opposite: entertainment, pleasure, diversion and escape from reality claim to make life good. Materialistic people ignore things, they avert their gaze when there are health problems or painful issues in the family or in the world around them. The world would prefer not to weep: it would rather ignore painful situations, cover them up, hide them. People spend so much energy on fleeing from situations of great suffering in the belief that reality can be dissimulated, situations where the cross would never, ever hide away.

A person who sees things as they truly are and suffers alongside those in pain and sorrow can experience the profundities of life and find true happiness. He or she is consoled not by the world but by Jesus. These people are not afraid of sharing the suffering of others, they do not flee from painful situations. And, in so doing, they discover that life has meaning when we assist those who suffer, when we understand their anguish, when we bring relief. These people recognize that because the other is of the same flesh, they are not afraid to approach and even touch the other's wounds; they feel so much compassion that all that separates them vanishes. In so doing, they embrace St. Paul's exhortation: "Mourn with those who mourn" (Rom. 12:15).

Knowing how to weep with others, this is what it means to be holy.

WHEN THE WORLD SEEMS LIKE A DESERT

How often the seeds of goodness and hope which we try to sow seem to get choked by weeds of selfishness, hostility and injustice—not just around us but in our own hearts. We are troubled by the growing gap in our societies between rich and poor. We detect signs of the idolatry of wealth, power and pleasure, which come at a high cost to human lives. Closer to home, many of our friends and peers suffer from spiritual poverty, loneliness and silent despair, even if they are surrounded by great material prosperity. God seems to be absent from the picture. It is as if a spiritual desert were slowly spreading through our world. It frequently strikes the young, robbing them of hope and, far too often, life itself.

And yet this is the world into which you are called to go forth and bear witness to the word of hope, to the Word of Jesus Christ and the promise of His kingdom.

A FAITHFUL FRIEND NEVER FAILS US

There is much to be learned from the prayer that has inspired us for the past eight centuries, the prayer that St. Francis composed at the end of his life: the *Canticle of Brother Sun*, also known as the *Canticle of the Creatures*. The Poverello did not write it during a time of joy or wellbeing. No, he was actually going through a period of great adversity. Francis was almost blind and weighed down by a burden of solitude that he had never before experienced. The world had not changed since he had started preaching, people continued to let themselves be torn apart by arguments and, moreover, he was well aware that his death was approaching. This could have been a time of great despair for him, he could have been greatly disillusioned, he could have felt as though he had failed. Instead, in those moments of sadness and during that very dark period of life, Francis prays. And how does he pray? "Praised be to You, our Lord..." He gives praise. Francis praises God for everything, for all the gifts of Creation, and even for death, which he courageously calls "Sister" or "Sister death." Francis, like other Christians, like Jesus, offers us an example: in moments of great difficulty, he praises God, opening the gates that lead down a great path toward the Lord, purifying us. Because praise always purifies.

The saints show us that we can always give praise, in good times and in bad, because God is our faithful Friend. This is the foundation of praise: God is our faithful Friend whose love never fails. He is always beside us. He always awaits us. Someone once said, "He is the sentinel by your side who keeps you moving forward with confidence." In dark and difficult times, let us find the courage to say, "Praised be to You, our Lord." Praise the Lord. It will do all of us so much good.

SEVEN

CULTIVATE KNOWLEDGE

LET US ASK FOR THE GIFT OF WISDOM IN OUR HEARTS

The Holy Spirit makes Christians "wise." This does not mean that they have an answer for everything or that they know everything but, to the degree that they "know about God," they know how God acts, they know when something pertains to God and when it does not. They have the wisdom that God places in our hearts. In this sense, the heart of a wise person has *all the characteristics of God*. How important it is that Christians like this live among us! Everything about them speaks of God, they are a beautiful and living sign of His presence and His love. This is not something we can invent or procure for ourselves: it is a gift that God grants those who open themselves up to the Holy Spirit. The Holy Spirit is in our hearts: we can choose to listen to Him or not. If we listen, He will show us the path of wisdom, the wisdom of seeing with God's eyes, hearing with God's ears, loving with God's heart, pronouncing on things with God's judgment. All of us can obtain it. We merely have to ask the Holy Spirit for it.

Think of a mother at home with her children, one child is doing one thing and the other is doing another; the poor mother must run back and forth between the two. When the mother gets tired and yells at them, is that wisdom? No, that is not wisdom. But when she takes the child and gently scolds him and says, "We do not do this," and patiently explains why—this is God's wisdom. It is the wisdom of the Holy Spirit. When a married couple argue and then do not look at each other for some time or only scowl at each other, is this God's wisdom? No, it is not! But if they say to each other, "Well, the problem is over, let us make peace now," and they move forward—this is the gift of wisdom.

It is something that cannot be learned; it is a gift of the Holy Spirit. This is why we must ask the Lord for the Holy Spirit and for the gift of *wisdom*. With this wisdom, we can move forward, build our family, build the Church and all will be sanctified.

GOD'S KNOWLEDGE OPENS US UP TO OTHERS

The only thing that gives us direction and sets us on the right path is knowledge, the *knowledge born of faith*. This is not the false knowledge of our world. It is the knowledge that we see in the eyes of parents and grandparents who have placed their trust in God. It is the light of God that we glimpse in their eyes, the light that they discovered in Jesus, which *is the knowledge of God* (cf. 1 Cor. 1:24).

This knowledge helps us recognize and *repel the false promises of happiness*. There are so many of them! A culture that offers false promises cannot free its people, it can only lead to an egoism that fills the heart with darkness and bitterness. The knowledge of God, on the other hand, helps us learn how to welcome and accept those who act and think differently than we do. It is sad when we close ourselves off in our small worlds and rely only on ourselves, when we espouse the principle of "my way or the highway." This is a bad principle and it does not help us. When we apply it to life we remain trapped, shut in on ourselves. When a people or religion or society become their own "small universe," they lose the best thing they have and endorse a mentality that is presumptuous, that of "I am good and you are bad." As a consequence of this way of thinking, we lose direction and ourselves—and life becomes meaningless.

The knowledge of God opens us up to others. It helps us look beyond our comfort zones and frees us from the false securities that make us blind to great ideals, the ideals that make life beautiful and worthy of being lived.

LISTEN TO THE HUMBLE

Among the female figures in the Old Testament one great heroine stands out: Judith. The biblical Book named after her recounts the massive military campaign of King Nebuchadnezzar who, while ruling over Nineveh, expands the boundaries of his empire by defeating and enslaving people who live in the surrounding area. This king is a great and invincible enemy who spreads death and destruction all the way to the Promised Land, endangering the lives of the children of Israel. In fact, Nebuchadnezzar's army, under the leadership of General Holofernes, lays siege to the Judean city of Bethulia and cuts off their water supply, thereby weakening the people's resistance.

The situation is so dramatic that the city's inhabitants plead with the elders to surrender to the enemy. They are desperate: "For now we have no one to help us; God has sold us into their hands, to strew us on the ground before them with thirst and utter destruction" (Judith. 7:25, RSV). They use those exact words: "God has sold us."

It is then that Judith appears on the scene. A widow and woman of great beauty and wisdom, she speaks to the people with the language of faith. Courageously, she reproaches them: "You are putting the Lord Almighty to the test—but you will never know anything! While we wait for his deliverance, let us call upon him to help us, and he will hear our voice, if it pleases him" (Judith. 8:13–17, RSV). With the strength of a prophet, Judith urges the men of her people to rediscover their faith in God; with the gaze of a prophet, she sees beyond the limited horizon proposed by the leaders, which fear limits even further. God will surely act.

The Lord is the God of Salvation, she believed, whatever form He may take. Salvation can bring life and liberation from one's enemies but, in His unknowable plans, salvation can also lead to death. As a woman of faith, she knows this. We know the ending of the story: God brings salvation.

Dear brothers and sisters, let us never impose conditions on God; let us instead allow hope to conquer our fears. Trusting in God means agreeing to His plans without expectations, accepting that His salvation and help might eventually come to us in unexpected ways. We ask the Lord for life, health, love and happiness—and so we should—but always with the awareness that God can also extract life from death, that we can feel peace even when we are ill, that we can feel tranquil even if we are lonely, that we can experience happiness even when we cry. It is not for us to instruct God what He should do or tell Him what we need. He knows it far better than we do and we must have faith in Him, because His path and thoughts are different from our own.

The path that Judith reveals to us is one of faith, of waiting peacefully, of prayer and of obedience. It is the path of hope. It means not surrendering immediately and doing everything we possibly can while always remaining in the trench cut by the Lord's will. As we know, Judith prayed a great deal, she spoke at length to many people, and then she courageously set out to reach the leader of the king's army to slit his throat and cut off his head. Judith shows courage in both faith and deed. She always seeks out the Lord! In fact, Judith has a plan of her own that she carries out successfully, leading her people to victory. She always shows the faith of one who accepts everything as it comes from the hand of God, certain of His goodness.

Judith is a woman full of faith and courage. She restores strength to her people, who are in mortal danger, and guides them down the path of hope, pointing it out to us along the way. If we stop to think about it, how often have we heard wise, courageous words from humble people, from humble women. Women who might otherwise be considered somewhat ignorant These are the words of God's wisdom!

THERE IS NO FUTURE THAT IS NOT TOGETHER

During the pandemic, we, like Thomas with his doubts and fears, experienced frailty. We needed the Lord; we needed the way He sees undeniable beauty beyond our frailty. We discovered that we are like beautiful crystals, both fragile and precious. Like crystals, we are transparent before Him and

His light, the light of mercy; it shines in us, through us and into the world. As Peter says, this is good reason to "greatly rejoice, though... you may have had to suffer grief in all kinds of trials" (1 Pet. 1:6).

The most beautiful message comes to us from the disciple who arrived late. Only Thomas was missing, but the Lord waited for Thomas. Mercy does not forget those who are delayed. And now, as we begin a slow and arduous phase of recovery from the pandemic, this is the danger: forgetting about those who are left behind. We risk being struck by an even worse virus: *selfish indifference.* This spreads by thinking that life is getting better for all if it is getting better for me; things will be all right if they are all right for me. This is how it begins. It ends by choosing some people over others, ignoring the poor, sacrificing those who are left behind on the altar of progress. The pandemic was a reminder that there are no differences or borders between those who suffer. We are all frail, we are all equal, we are all precious. We should have been moved to act by what was happening: the time has come to do away with inequality; we need to heal the injustices that undermine the health of humanity! Let us learn from the early Christians as described in the Acts of the Apostles. They received mercy and they lived with mercy: "All the believers were together and had all in common; they sold property and possessions to give to anyone who had need" (Acts 2:44–45). This is not mere ideology. This is Christianity.

In that community, after the resurrection of Jesus, only one was left behind and the others waited for him. Today the opposite seems to be true: a small fraction of humanity has moved ahead, while the majority has remained behind. Each of us could easily say, "These are complex problems, it is not my job to take care of the needy, others should take care of them!" St. Faustina, after finding Jesus, wrote: "In a suffering soul, we should see Jesus Crucified, and not a loafer or a burden on the community... Lord, You give us occasion to practice deeds of mercy, and instead we use the occasions to pass judgment."* Even so, one day she complained to Jesus that people who were merciful were thought of as naive. "Lord, they often take advantage of my goodness," she said. And Jesus replied: "That makes no difference, my daughter, that is no concern of yours. As for you, be always merciful toward other people, and especially sinners."† I say to everyone, let us not think only of our interests, our vested interests. Let us welcome this trial as an opportunity to prepare for our collective future, a future for all, no one excluded. Without a vision for all, there will be a future for no one.

LET YOURSELF BE LOVED

Try and sit still for a moment and let yourself be loved by God. Try and silence all the noise within and rest for a few moments in His loving embrace. When He asks something of you, or simply presents you with one of life's challenges, He hopes you will make room for Him so He can encourage you to grow. He does not mind if you share your doubts with Him; on the contrary, He is concerned when you do not talk to Him, when you do not communicate openly with Him. His

---

* *Diary of Saint Maria Faustina Kowalska, Divine Mercy in My Soul* (2005), https://liturgicalyear.files.wordpress.com/2012/10/divine-mercy-in-my-soul.pdf; 6 September 1937, v. 1268.
† Ibid., 24 December 1937 v. 1446.

love is so real, true and concrete that it invites us into a relationship of openness and fruitful dialogue. In short, seek the closeness of your heavenly Father in the loving countenances of His courageous witnesses on earth!

QUICKSAND

Conversion leads us to suffer for the sins we have committed, to feel desire to be free of them and the will to exclude them from one's life forever. To stop sinning, one must reject everything connected to sin. This means that it is necessary to reject a materialistic mentality, an excessive interest in comfort, and an excessive interest in pleasure, wellbeing and wealth. The first aspect of conversion is *detachment from sin and materialism*. We begin the journey with detachment from these things.

The other aspect of conversion is the goal of the journey: the *search for God and His kingdom*. We detach from temporal things to search for God and His kingdom. Casting aside comfort and materialism is not an end in itself. It is not an ascesis in the name of penance: a Christian is not a "fakir." This is different. Detachment is not an end in itself but a means of attaining something greater, namely, the kingdom of God, communion with God, friendship with God. But this is not easy. There are many ties that bind us closely to sin and temptation is always there, tugging on us, pulling us down. There are so many ties that link us to sin: inconstancy, discouragement, malice, toxic environments, bad examples. Sometimes, the connection we feel with the Lord is so weak it seems like God is silent; His promises of consolation seem remote and unreal. In such times we are tempted to say that it

CULTIVATE KNOWLEDGE

is impossible to truly convert. How often we have heard this kind of discouragement!

"No, I cannot do it. I try but then I have to give up." While this is unfortunate, it happens. When you have discouraging thoughts like that, do not sit still. These thoughts can be like quicksand, the quicksand of a mediocre existence. This is mediocrity. What can we do when we would like to move forward but feel as though we cannot? First of all, we need to remind ourselves that conversion is a grace: it does not depend on strength alone. It is a grace granted by the Lord and we need to ask God for it forcefully. We need to ask God to convert us, we need to believe we can open ourselves up to the beauty, the goodness and the tenderness of God. Think of God's tenderness. God is not a bad father, He is not unkind. He is tender, He loves us a great deal, like the Good Shepherd who searches for the missing members of His flock. God is love. And this is conversion: a grace of God. Set off on your journey, for He is the One who inspires. You will see Him coming toward you. He will be there. Pray, take a step, keep walking.

A CHRISTIAN'S PLAN OF ACTION

Please do not "blend" your faith in Jesus Christ with other things. You can have blended fruit drinks—orange, apple, banana—but please do not drink a "blended" form of faith. Faith is whole and complete, it should not be blended. It is faith in Jesus. It is faith in the Son of God made man, who loves me and who died for me. Make yourselves heard and tend to the two extremities of society: the elderly and the young. Do not let yourselves be excluded and do not let the elderly be excluded. Secondly: do not "blend" your faith in Jesus Christ.

"What should we do then, Father?" you ask. Read the Beatitudes, for they will do you good. If you want to know exactly what you should do, read Matthew Chapter 25, which describes the standards by which we shall be judged. These two things will provide you with a plan of action: the Beatitudes and Matthew 25. You do not need to read anything else. But, with all my heart, I ask you: do not blend your faith.

KEEP THE FAITH!

Prayer leads us to trust in God even in times of difficulty. It helps us find hope when there seems to be none. It sustains us in our everyday struggles. Prayer is not an escape, not a way of running away from our problems. On the contrary, it is the only weapon at our disposal for keeping love and hope alive when we are surrounded by so many weapons of death. It is not easy to raise our eyes to the heavens when we are hurting, but faith helps us resist the temptation of relying solely on ourselves. We may want to get angry and cry out to God in our pain. We should not be afraid to do so, for this is also a form of prayer. An elderly woman once said to her grandchildren: "Even getting angry with God is a kind of prayer." This is the wisdom of the simple and just, for they know how to raise their eyes heavenward in times of hardship... Sometimes God even hears this kind of prayer better than others precisely because it comes from a wounded heart. The Lord always hears the cries of His people and He dries their tears. Dear brothers and sisters, do not stop raising your eyes toward heaven. Keep the faith!

CULTIVATE KNOWLEDGE

BECOME A STAR AND SHINE WITH THE LIGHT OF CHRIST

How does the light of Christ shine everywhere and always? It has its own way of irradiating light. It does not rely on the powerful media empires of this world, who are always trying to seize more power. No. The light of Christ spreads by proclaiming the Word of God, by proclaiming faith, by speaking the Word, by bearing witness, and by the same "method" that God chose to appear among us: through incarnation, which is to say by standing alongside someone, encountering the other, sharing the other's reality and bearing the witness of our faith. Every single one of us. This is the only way that the light of Christ, which is love, can shine in those who welcome it, and thereby attract others with it. The light of Christ does not expand with words alone, or through artificial, commercial methods. No. Proclaiming faith, sharing the Word of God and bearing witness: this is how the light of Christ expands. The star is Christ but we, too, can and should be stars for our brothers and our sisters, bearing witness of the treasures of goodness and the infinite mercy that the Redeemer offers freely to everyone. The light of Christ does not expand through proselytizing but by bearing witness and by confessing our faith. And through martyrdom, too.

We need to welcome this light and constantly make more room for it. But heads up lest we think it can be possessed! Heads up lest we think it simply needs to be managed!

A SAD FAITH...BETTER OFF WITHOUT IT!

The journey of joy is not a stroll in the park. It takes hard work to always be joyful. John left behind everything when he was young to put God first, to listen to the Word of God with all his heart and strength. John withdrew into the desert and stripped himself of all superfluous things so that he could be freer to follow the breeze of the Holy Spirit. Unquestionably, some aspects of John's personality are unique and inimitable, definitely not for everyone. But his testimony stands as a paradigm for those who seek the meaning of life and true joy. Specifically, John the Baptist is a good model for those in the Church who feel the calling to proclaim Christ to others. They can only do it by detaching from themselves and the secular world; it cannot be done by attracting people to themselves but by directing others toward Jesus. This is joy: directing people toward Jesus. And our faith must know joy. Even in dark moments, we must have that inner joy of knowing that the Lord is with us, that the Lord is risen. The Lord! This is the center of our life and the center of our joy. Think carefully: How am I behaving? Am I a joyful person who knows how to transmit the joy of being Christian? Or am I always glum, do I always seem like I am at a wake? If I do not have the joy of faith, I cannot bear witness, and when people see a lack of joy, they will say, "If faith is so sad, I'm better off without it."

LET US NOT BE AFRAID OF BEING TRUTHFUL

I believe we all know what the word hypocrisy means. What is hypocrisy? When we say, "Be careful, that person is a hypocrite," what are we trying to say? What is hypocrisy? We could say it is the fear of the truth. Hypocrites are afraid of the truth. They prefer to pretend rather than truly be themselves. It is like putting makeup on your soul, like putting makeup on your behavior, putting makeup on your path forward: it is not the truth. Pretending stops people from speaking the truth. It is a way out of having to always speak the truth, everywhere and always. Pretending leads to half-truths. And half-truths are a sham because either something is the truth or it is not. Half-truths are an untrue way of behaving. We prefer to pretend rather than be ourselves. Pretense prevents us from having to find the courage to speak the truth openly. Thus, we get out of the obligation—following the commandment—to speak the truth, always and everywhere. And in an environment where interpersonal relations are lived under the aegis of formalism, the virus of hypocrisy spreads with ease. We see this in smiles that do not come from the heart, from people who seem to get along with everyone but really get along with no one.

Hypocrites are people who pretend, flatter and deceive because they live under a mask and do not have the courage to face the truth. For this reason, they are incapable of truly loving: hypocrites do not know how to love. Their lives are built on ego and they do not have the strength to reveal what is in their hearts. There are many situations where we see hypocrisy at work. We often find it in the workplace, where people try and be amicable with colleagues, while competition leads them to stab those same people in the back. In the realm of politics, it is not unusual to find hypocrites who live one way in public and another way in private. Hypocrisy in the Church is particularly odious but unfortunately it exists; there are many hypocritical Christians and ministers. We should never forget the Lord's words: "All you need to say is simply 'Yes' or 'No'; anything beyond this comes from the evil one" (Matt. 5:37). Brothers and sisters, let us not be afraid to be truthful, to speak the truth, to hear the truth, to live in the truth. In so doing, we will be able to love. A hypocrite does not know how to love.

GOD IS OUR DAILY BREAD, NOT A SIDE DISH

It would be more convenient for us if God stayed up in heaven and did not get involved in our lives so that we could take care of things down here on earth. However, God made Himself man so He could enter into the concrete reality of this world, to enter into our reality; God made Himself man for you and me, for all of us, to be part of our lives. He is interested in all aspects of our lives. We can talk to Him about our feelings, work, how our day went, our suffering, pain, any number of things. We can tell Him everything; Jesus wants this kind of intimacy with us. What does He not want? He does not want to be considered a side dish. He is our daily bread. He does not want to be overlooked and set aside, or to be called on only when we need Him.

RESIST THE TEMPTATION OF THINKING ABOUT YOURSELF

"Save yourself!" (Mark 15:30). This common temptation spares no one, including us Christians. It is the temptation to think only of saving ourselves or those who are part of our group, to focus on our problems and interests alone, as if nothing else mattered. It is a very human instinct but it is wrong. It represents the final temptation of crucified God.

1. **Ordinary people**
   Save yourself. The first to say these words were "those who passed by" (Mark 15:29). They were ordinary people. They had heard Jesus teach and witnessed His miracles. They say to Him, "Come down from the cross and save yourself" (Mark 15:30). They did not feel pity, they only wanted miracles. It is probable that we, too, at times would prefer a god who works wonders rather than one who is compassionate, a god who communicates power, who shows his might and does away with those who wish us harm. But that is not God. That is our ego speaking. We would rather have a god that looks like us rather than have to work to become like Him. We want a god like us, rather than having to become like God!

2. **Leaders**
   Save yourself. The next people to say these words were the leaders: the head priests and scribes. They condemned Jesus because they considered Him dangerous. We are all good at crucifying others to save ourselves. Jesus, however, let Himself be crucified to teach us not to blame evil on others. Those religious leaders accused Him precisely because of what He had done for others: "He saved others...but he can't save himself!" (Mark 15:31). They knew who Jesus was, they remembered how He had healed some people and freed others and they came to their malicious conclusions about Him. They insinuated that saving and helping others brought about no good; Jesus, who gave of Himself for others, would die! They cloak their mockery with religious terms, using the verb *to save* twice.

But the "gospel" of *saving yourself* is not the Gospel of salvation. It is the falsest of the apocryphal gospels because it forces others to carry the cross. The true Gospel bids us take up the cross of others.

3. **The condemned**

    Save yourself. At the end, even those who were crucified with Jesus joined in the taunting against Him. How easy it is to criticize, to speak against others, to point to evil in others but not in ourselves, even to blame the weak and the outcast! Why did those men on the cross get angry with Jesus? Because He did not help them down from the cross. "Save yourself and us!" they say (Luke 23:39). They looked to Jesus for a resolution to their problems. But God does not come to us just to free us from our problems, which continue to present themselves on a daily basis, but to free us from the real problem, which is the lack of love.

Dear brothers and sisters, Calvary was the site of a great duel: between God—who came to save us—and man—who wants to only save himself; between faith in God and the cult of the self; between man who accuses and God who excuses. God was victorious and His mercy descended over earth.

EIGHT

DO NOT WATCH LIFE GO BY FROM A BALCONY

IF YOU ARE LOOKING FOR GOD IN AN ARMCHAIR OR IN THE MIRROR, YOU WILL NEVER FIND HIM

How do we hear the Lord? How do we hear Him? Where does the Lord speak? Do you have the Lord's mobile phone number? How do we hear the Lord? I can tell you this and I mean it: we do not hear the Lord while sitting *in an armchair*. Do you understand? If you spend your time sitting in a cozy armchair, doing nothing and hoping to hear the Lord, I can assure you that you will hear everything but the Lord. You cannot hear the Lord while living a comfortable life. If you live life sitting down, statically—and this is very important—there will be interference and you will not hear the Word of God, which is dynamic. The Word of God is not static; if you are static, you will not be able to hear Him. You can find God if you are in movement, if you are *walking*. If you are not walking toward something, working for others, bearing witness, doing kind acts, you will never hear the Lord. To hear the Lord, you must be in movement, you cannot sit around waiting for something to magically happen.

Jesus gives us advice on how to hear the voice of the Lord: "Seek, and you will find" (Luke 11:9). All right, but where should I look? Not on your mobile phone, as I have already said. Calls from the Lord will not reach us on our mobile phones. Not on television; the Lord does not own a channel. Definitely not in loud and disorienting music and entertainment: you will not find a connection to heaven there. Nor will you find the Lord standing in front of your mirror, you will only be disappointed to see yourself. The only questions you should ask yourself while standing in front of the mirror are things like, "Who am I? What am I doing here? What should I do now?" You may even experience that familiar kind of bitterness that leads us to sadness. No, you must continue moving. Do not look for Him in the safety of your room, closed in on yourselves, mulling over the past or daydreaming about the future. God speaks to us in relation to others, in movement. Do not hide away: trust in Him, entrust everything to Him, seek Him out in prayer, seek Him out while speaking with others, look for Him while on your journey.

DIGITAL SPACES VERSUS REAL LIFE

A document penned by three hundred young people around the world pointed out that "online relationships can become inhuman. Digital spaces blind us to the vulnerability of others and stop us from practicing self-reflection. Problems like pornography distort a young person's perception of human sexuality. Technology used in this way creates a delusional parallel reality that pays no mind to human dignity."* For many people, an immersion into the virtual world has led to a kind of "digital migration," distancing them from their families and cultural-religious values, bringing them into a lonely world of self-invention, and making them feel rootless even though they remain physically in one place. Young people today, whom we are used to seeing as lively, exuberant and eager to affirm their personality, have a new challenge: interacting with a virtual world that they have to face all on their own, as if exploring a new continent. Today's youth is the first generation forced to process and synthesize information that is simultaneously personal, cultural and global. To do this effectively they need to shift from connecting virtually to communicating in a healthy and decisive manner.

AN INVASION OF PRIVACY

Oddly enough, while attitudes of closure and intolerance are on the rise, distances are shrinking or even disappearing to the extent that the right to privacy barely exists anymore. Everything has become a spectacle that can be spied on and observed; people's lives are under constant surveillance. Digital communication seeks to bring everything out into the open; people's lives are combed over, laid bare and shared, often anonymously. In so doing, respect for others disintegrates. Even as we decline, ignore or block others, we can still peer shamelessly into every detail of their lives.

---

* A document created at the Pre-Synodal meeting March 19–24 2018.

BRIDGES DO NOT GET BUILT ONLINE

Digital media can expose people to a number of risks: addiction, isolation and the gradual loss of contact with reality, thereby blocking the development of authentic interpersonal skills. Relationships need physical gestures, facial expressions, moments of silence, body language, even odors, trembling hands, blushing, perspiration—all of that is part and parcel of human communications. Digital relationships lack all the complexities involved in building a friendship, they are not a stable form of interaction and they do not foster consensus, which takes time to mature. They are social in semblance only. They do not build community. Rather, they offer a disguise, they build on the individualism that finds expression in xenophobia and in contempt for the vulnerable. A digital connection does not build bridges and cannot unite humanity.

NOT EVERYTHING IS A "LIKE/DISLIKE"

True wisdom demands an encounter with reality. Today, however, reality can be manufactured, faked, modified. A direct encounter with reality can prove intolerable. Consequently, a mechanism of "selection" comes into play, whereby I immediately separate what I like from what I dislike, what I consider attractive from what I deem distasteful. In much the same way, we can choose the people with whom we wish to share our world. In today's virtual networks, people or situations we find unpleasant or disagreeable are simply deleted. This creates a virtual circle that serves to isolate us further from the real world.

The ability to sit down and listen to others has become emblematic of a warm welcoming attitude. Sitting down and truly listening to another person, a distinctive quality of any human encounter, offers up a paradigm for how to welcome people warmly, how to go beyond a narcissistic attitude and be receptive, how to make room for them in our circles.

With the disappearance of silence and attentive listening—which has been replaced by a frenzy of swift and impatient messaging—the basic structure of all wise human communication is at risk. A new lifestyle is emerging, one in which we create only what we want and exclude everything we cannot control or understand instantly and superficially. This process, by logical extension, blocks the serene reflection that can lead to shared wisdom.

We should instead seek the truth in dialogue, relaxed conversation and passionate debate. This path calls for perseverance, it includes moments of silence and suffering but, ultimately, it will unite the broad experiences of many individuals and peoples.

WILLING TO ENCOUNTER EACH OTHER BEYOND THE WEB

The ocean of information at our fingertips does not lead to greater wisdom. Wisdom cannot be manufactured through rapid searches on the internet; wisdom is not a mass of unverified data. It is definitely not how we mature in an encounter with truth. Online conversations end up revolving only around the latest data; they are merely layered and cumulative. We fail to focus intently, we do not delve into the heart of matters or recognize what is essential, which would give meaning to our lives. Because of this, freedom has become an illusion that we are peddled, one that is easily confused with the ability to navigate the internet. The path to fellowship, whether local or universal, can only be undertaken by free spirits, those who are willing to experience true encounters.

WHAT ROBOTS DO NOT KNOW HOW TO DO

The other day, while discussing Artificial Intelligence, someone asked if AI would one day be able to do everything. They specifically wanted to know if the robots of the future would be able to do everything that a person can do. "What won't they be able to do?" I asked. They thought for a minute and then said, "There is only one thing they will never have: tenderness." Tenderness is like hope. It is, as the poet Charles Péguy describes it, a virtue of the humble. These kinds of virtues are linked to gentleness, they do not declaim or declare.

With regards to an ecological conversion, I believe—and I want to stress this—that we need to work on our human ecology. We need to work on tenderness, on our capability for being gentle. We have to work on being kinder: it is a quality that is tied to living well and in harmony with others.

A GREAT STEP FOR MANKIND

When man first walked on the moon, he said a phrase that became famous: "That's one small step for man, one giant leap for mankind." It was indeed a historical achievement for humanity. But with Mary's Assumption into heaven we celebrate an infinitely greater conquest. The Virgin Mary walked into paradise: she went there not only in spirit but with her body as well, with all of herself. The lowly Virgin of Nazareth took one small step that was a huge leap forward for mankind. Going to the moon has little meaning if we cannot live as brothers and sisters on this earth. But the fact that one of us dwells in the flesh in heaven gives us hope: we understand that we are precious and destined to rise again. God does not allow our bodies to disappear into nothingness. With God, nothing is lost! Through Mary, our goal was reached. We understand why we are on this path: not to gain earthly things, which vanish, but to gain access to heaven, which is eternal.

DO NOT BE A PHOTOCOPY; BE YOURSELF

It is true that the digital world can expose you to the risk of isolating yourself and seeking out empty pleasures. But let us not forget that there are also young people who work in this field who show creativity and genius. Such is the case of young Carlo Acutis. Carlo was well aware that the whole apparatus of communication, advertising and social networking can be used to lull us to sleep, make us addicted to consumerism, obsessed with how we spend our free time, and trap us in negativity. But he also knew how to use communication technology to transmit the Word, to communicate values and beauty.

Although Carlo did not fall into the trap, he saw many young people who—even though they wanted to be different—ended up behaving just like everyone else, chasing after whatever those in power dangled before them, all because of the power of consumerism and distraction. In so doing, those people did not cultivate the gifts the Lord gave them and did not offer the world those unique personal talents that God granted them. As Carlo pointed out, "People are born originals but many die as photocopies." Don't let this happen to you!

Don't let them rob you of hope and joy, or drug you into becoming a slave to their interests. Dare to be more. Your being is more precious than any possession that exists. You do not only need to possess or appear to. You can become what God your Creator knows you are, if you only accept that you are being called to something greater. Ask the Holy Spirit for help and stride with confidence towards the great goal of holiness. In this way, you will not be a photocopy. You will be completely yourself.

NINE

GET YOUR HANDS DIRTY

COME TO TERMS WITH YOUR FEARS

What are you afraid of? What worries you most deeply? An "underlying" fear that many young people have is that of not being loved, liked or accepted. Many young people today feel as though they have to be different from who they really are in an attempt to adapt to often artificial and unattainable standards. They continuously retouch their photographs, hide behind masks and false identities, and almost become fakes themselves. Many are obsessed with receiving "likes." Countless fears and uncertainties stem from this sense of inadequacy. Others are afraid that they will never find emotional security and that they will always be alone. Many, faced with uncertain employment, fear they will never find satisfying or secure jobs and that they will never be able to fulfill their dreams. These fears strike high numbers of young people today, both believers and non-believers. Indeed, even those who have accepted the gift of faith and seek their vocation seriously are not exempt from such fears. Some think,

"Maybe God will ask too much of me; maybe if I follow the path He has shown me, I will not be happy, or I will not be able to do everything He asks of me." Others may think, "If I start to follow the path that God has shown me, how do I know I will be able to follow it all the way through? Maybe I will get discouraged and lose enthusiasm... Will I be able to persevere for the whole of my life?" Ask yourself difficult questions: what upsets you most? What are you most afraid of? What blocks you and stops you from moving forward? Why do you lack the courage to make the choices you need to make? Do not be afraid to face your fears honestly, to recognize them for what they are and to come to terms with them.

SMALL STEPS FOR BECOMING BETTER

We can all ask ourselves the following questions: How have I responded to the Lord's call to holiness? Do I want to get stronger, do better, be more Christian? This is the path to holiness. When the Lord invites us to become saints, He is not forcing us to do something oppressive or sad—quite the contrary! He is inviting us to share in His joy, to live in joy every single moment of our lives by transforming those moments into a gift of love to share with the people around us. If we can comprehend this, everything will change and take on new meaning, and it will be beautiful. Small, everyday things will be the first to change. For example, a lady goes to the market to buy some groceries and bumps into a neighbor. They begin to talk and soon start gossiping. But the first lady says, "No, no, I do not want to speak badly about anyone." This is a first step toward sainthood, it helps you become more holy. Or else, you go home after work and your son wants to talk a little about his dreams and ideas. You would like to say, "Oh, I am so tired, I worked so hard today..." but instead you sit down and listen to your son patiently because it is good for him. This, too, is a step toward holiness. Or else we finally reach the end of the day but still make the time to say our prayers. Or we go to Mass on Sundays and receive Communion, but not before engaging in a strong confession, which cleans us up a little. These are all steps in the direction of sainthood. We ponder the Virgin Mary, who was so good and beautiful, and we pick up our rosaries and pray. That is another step toward sainthood. I go out in the street, I see a poor person in need, I stop and talk to him and give him something: this is a step in the direction of sainthood.

While these are small things, they are all steps toward sainthood. Each step makes us better people, liberates us from selfishness and helps us step outside of ourselves and become more receptive to our brothers and sisters and their needs.

WHO DO YOU WANT TO RESEMBLE?

The "rest" that Christ offers to the weary and oppressed is not just psychological solace or charity, but the joy of the poor when they are evangelized and become builders of the new humanity. This is the solace and joy that Jesus grants us. It is unique, it is His own joy. It is a message for all of us, for all people of goodwill, a message that Jesus continues to convey while the world around us continues to exalt those who become rich and powerful. How often we say to ourselves, "Oh, I wish I could be like him or her, they are rich, they have so much power, they lack for nothing." The world exalts the rich and powerful with any and all means, often trampling the dignity of human beings. We see these trampled people every day. And this is a message for the Church, too. To do works of mercy and evangelize the poor, She should be meek and humble. This is how the Lord wants His Church—which is to say, us—to be.

ONLY LOVE CAN HEAL LIFE

Sisters and brothers, let Jesus look upon and heal your hearts. I need to do this, too! I need to let Jesus look upon my heart and heal it. If you have already felt His gentle gaze upon you, imitate Him, do as He does. Look around: you will see many people who feel wounded and alone, people who need to feel loved. Take the step. Jesus asks you to look but do not stop at outward appearances, look upon their hearts but do not be judgmental. Let us stop judging others and welcome people in. Let us open our hearts so we can welcome in others. Only love heals life.

GOD IS COMMITTED TO YOU; ARE YOU COMMITTED TO HIM?

I would like to pause briefly and reflect on the theme of commitment. What is commitment? What does it mean to be committed? When I commit to something, it means that I assume a responsibility, I carry out a task for someone. Commitment also has to do with the manner with which I dedicate myself to and show my faith, the care with which I carry out the task. We are constantly asked to commit to things: prayer, work, study, sport, recreation... Committing to something means putting great effort and strength into improving life.

God committed Himself to us. And in what do we see His commitment? We can read about it in the Bible. Through Jesus, God committed Himself to restoring hope: to the poor, to those deprived of dignity, to foreigners, to the sick, to prisoners and sinners, whom He embraced with kindness. Jesus was always the living expression of the Father's mercy. This is God's commitment, this is why He sent us Jesus. He wanted to draw closer to us, all of us, and open the door of His love, His heart, His mercy. And this is truly very beautiful!

Jesus expressed God's commitment with His merciful love. We can and should reciprocate His love with our commitment, especially in situations of dire need, where there is an even greater hunger for hope. We need, for example, to commit to those who are ignored, to those with severe disabilities, to the seriously ill, to the dying, to those who are unable to express gratitude... In all these situations we can convey God's mercy through our commitment, which bears witness to our faith in Christ. We must always carry God's gentle caress—God caressed us with His mercy—to others, to those who suffer in their hearts or are sad: we need to approach them with God's caress, the very same that He gave to us.

BE LIKE SAINTS, WHEREVER YOU ARE!

You do not need to be a bishop, priest or member of a religious order to be holy. We are inclined to think that holiness is something that pertains to those who do not have to engage in everyday matters, who can spend a great deal of time in prayer. This is not the case. We are called on to be holy by living our lives with love and by bearing witness in everything we do, wherever we may be. Are you a member of a religious order? Be holy by living out your commitment joyfully. Are you married? Be holy by loving and caring for your husband or wife, as Christ did for the Church. Are you part of the labor force? Be holy by working with integrity and skill in the service of your brothers and sisters. Are you a parent or grandparent? Be holy by patiently teaching your little ones how to follow Jesus. Are you in a position of authority? Be holy by working for the common good and by renouncing personal gain.

IT IS NOT ENOUGH TO SAY, "MAY GOD HELP YOU"

At the end of the day, Jesus asks the disciples to feed the multitudes. Why does He make this request? It stems from two facts: the crowd and the disciples. The crowd has followed Jesus and finds itself outdoors, in a remote place, far from any villages, with night falling; the disciples are worried about the crowd and ask Jesus to disperse them so each person can go find food and lodgings (cf. Luke. 9:12). Faced with the problematic needs of the crowd, this is the disciples' solution: disperse them and each man for himself! Each man for himself! How often we Christians give in to this temptation! We ignore the needs of others and dismiss them with a pious "May God help you" or with an even less pious "Good luck to you." But Jesus comes up with a different kind of solution, one that surprises the disciples. "Give them something to eat," He says (Luke 9:13). But how can we feed a crowd, the disciples ask. "We have only five loaves of bread and two fish—unless we go and buy food for all this crowd" (Luke 9:13). But Jesus does not despair. As we read in the Scripture, He asks the disciples to seat the people in groups of fifty, He looks to heaven, recites the blessing, breaks the bread and gives it to the disciples to distribute (cf. Luke 9:16). It is a moment of deep communion: the thirst of the crowd is quenched by the Word of God and their hunger is satiated by His Bread of Life. Everyone is nourished.

A FRESH COAT OF PAINT IS NOT ENOUGH

We need real men and women, not people who pretend to be men and women. True men and women, who speak up against criminality and exploitation. Do not be afraid to accuse and denounce! We need men and women who live free, who love the weakest among us and who are passionate about legality, reflecting their inner honesty. We need men and women who do what they say and who say no to *gattopardismo*, merely shuffling things around without really changing things. I have to work hard at my commitments, not simply whitewash things and move on. No, a fresh coat of paint is not enough. Life is commitment, struggling, speaking up, debating, putting your life on the line for something you believe in, dreaming…

A GOOD CHRISTIAN

Yesterday a good man, a factory-owner, came to Mass at Saint Martha House. Unfortunately, this man can no longer keep his factory open and has been forced to shut it down; this fact brought him to tears. "It is hard for me to take work away from fifty families. It is easy for me: I can declare bankruptcy and go home with money, but my heart will weep for these fifty families for the rest of my life." This is a good Christian: he prays through deeds, he came to Mass to ask the Lord for a way out, and not just for him but for the fifty families he employed. This is a man who knows how to pray, both with his heart and through deeds. He is in a difficult situation. He is not seeking the easy way out, he does not say, "Let them figure things out on their own." This is a true Christian. It did me good to meet with him! And surely, with the employment troubles we are experiencing today, with so much suffering, there are many like him.

IMMUNITY AGAINST SADNESS

With Jesus, we can become immune to sadness. While we will never forget our failures, troubles, problems or unmet dreams, the weight of them cannot crush us because Jesus is there, beneath it all, encouraging us with His love.

A LOVE THAT DOES NOT DECEIVE

To love *in the same way* that Jesus Christ did means doing service, putting yourself at the service of your brothers and sisters, just as He did when He washed the feet of the disciples. It also means stepping outside of ourselves, stepping away from our certainties, leaving behind earthly comforts and opening our hearts to others, especially those in need. It means making ourselves available both with what we are and what we have. This means loving not with words but with deeds.

To love in a Christlike manner means saying no to other "loves" that the world offers us: money—those who love money do not love in the same way that Jesus does—or success, vanity, power... These paths of "love" are deceptive, they lead us away from the Lord's love and make us selfish, narcissistic and aggressive. Aggression leads to a degeneration of love, to the abuse of others and to the suffering of loved ones. I think here of how unhealthy love turns into violence—how many women today are victims of violence... This is not love. To love as the Lord loves us means appreciating those who stand alongside us, respecting their freedom, loving them as they are and not as we would want them to be—as they are, unconditionally. Ultimately, Jesus asks us to abide in His love, to dwell in His love, and not in our ideas, not in self-worship. Those who dwell in self-worship live in the mirror and are always looking at themselves. He asks us to overcome the desire to control and manage others and serve them instead. We need to open our hearts to others; this is love.

IMMERSE YOURSELF IN LIFE

It is not up to others to be the protagonists of change. You are the ones who hold the future! You! The future enters the world through you. I ask you to be the protagonists of this transformation. Fight apathy by offering a Christian response to the social and political ills that exist in various parts of the world. Be builders and work hard to build a better world. Please, do not stand on your balconies and peer down on life. Jesus did not watch life unfold from a balcony, He immersed Himself in life. You, too, should immerse yourselves in life, just as Jesus did.

TEN

NEVER ALONE AGAIN

DIALOGUE CONNECTS US

Approaching someone, speaking to them, listening to them, observing them, getting to know and understand them and finding common ground: all these can be summed up with one word: "dialogue." If we want to encounter and help each other, we have to engage in dialogue. There is no need for me to stress the benefits of dialogue. All I have to do is think of what the world would be like without the gentle dialogue of the generous people who keep families and communities together. Persistent and courageous dialogue does not make headlines and yet it helps the world live so much better than we can possibly imagine.

A CONNECTED WORLD... WHERE WE ARE ALL DISTANT

Today everything seems connected but, in actual fact, we often feel isolated and distant from one another. I would like each of you to reflect on the solitude that resides in your heart: how many times do you find yourself feeling sad because of that solitude? This feeling acts like a thermometer and if you are sad, the temperature—the good deeds we do, how we welcome others, if we are getting our hands dirty—is too low. Sadness is an indicator of a lack of commitment and without commitment you will never be able to *be builders of the future*! But *you must* become a builder of the future: it is in your hands! You cannot simply pick up a telephone and call a company to come and build it. You have the opportunity to build the future: with your heart, love, passions, dreams. With other people. At the service of others. Think about this carefully: the future is in *your* hands.

THE COURAGE OF SHARING THE SORROW OF OTHERS

Compassion is not a material sensation; true compassion means suffering alongside someone, taking on the sorrows of others. Perhaps it would do us good to ask ourselves: Do I have compassion? Do I feel compassion for the people who suffer because of war, famine or pandemics? Do I feel compassion toward my brethren? Am I capable of suffering with them? Or do I look the other way? Do I say, "Let them fend for themselves"? Let us not forget the importance of the word *compassion*: it is trust in the providential love of the Father and it signifies sharing with courage.

STARVING FOR LOVE

You will surely become men and women devoted to the Christian encounter. Today's world is a place of civil unrest and wars, a place where it is hard to understand people. Your vocation will be to both meet people and have people meet, to encourage encounters between people. Faith is based on an encounter, an encounter with God. God did not leave us alone, He came toward us. He came to encounter us; He made the first move toward an encounter. And in the encounter between us, what importance does the dignity of others have? God wants us to save ourselves together, not alone. He wants us to be happy together, not egoistically on our own. He wants us to save ourselves as a people. Integration, outreach, solidarity and respect for the dignity of others are not just values of well-mannered people, but the characteristics of a Christian. A Christian who is not supportive is not a Christian. What is lacking today, what people are starving for, is love. Not sentimental love like that of a soap opera, but real love, like that in the Scripture. And so I ask each one of you: How is your love? What does the thermometer of your love say?

ECSTASY AND COMMUNION

When an encounter with God is called an "ecstasy," it is because it takes us out of ourselves and raises us up—we are stunned by God's love and beauty. However, we can also experience ecstasy when we recognize hidden beauty in others, their dignity, their grandeur in the image of God and children of the Father. This is why it is always better to live the faith together, express our love in a community, and share our affection, time, faith and troubles.

WHEN A BRICK IS WORTH MORE THAN A HUMAN BEING

I remember a medieval tale that describes the construction of a tower. The workers were all slaves: if one of them fell and died, no one said a thing. At the most they would say, "Poor man, he made a mistake and fell." Instead, if a brick fell and broke, everyone complained loudly. And the person responsible was punished. Why? Because bricks were expensive to craft, shape and cook. Making bricks took time and effort. A brick was worth more than a human being. In today's world, things like this still happen. Shares in the financial markets fall and the papers are filled with the news. Thousands of people continuously fall to their death due to hunger and poverty and no one says a thing.

IT IS NOT ENOUGH TO NOT DO HARM

We sometimes think that being Christian means doing no harm. Not doing harm is certainly good, but not doing good is unacceptable. We must do good acts, step outside ourselves, look around and see the people in need. There is so much hunger, even in the hearts of our cities. And yet how often do we fall prey to indifference: we see a poor person and look away. Reach out to that poor person, for he is Christ. Some people say, "All these priests and bishops go on and on about the poor, always the poor...But we want them to talk about eternal life!" Sisters and brothers, the poor are at the heart of the Bible. Jesus taught us to speak to the poor. Jesus came for the poor. Reach out to the poor. You have so much and yet you let your brother and sister die of hunger?

Dear brothers and sisters, let the teaching of Jesus echo in your heart. "Reach out to the poor," Jesus said. He also said, "I am the poor."

EVERY DAY IS AN OPPORTUNITY

Every passing day brings us new opportunities, new possibilities. We should not expect those who govern to do everything, for this would be childish. We have the privilege of sharing the responsibility, we can set up and generate new processes and bring about change. Let us take an active role in renewing and supporting our troubled societies. Today we have ample opportunity to express our innate congeniality, to be Good Samaritans and assume the pain of other people's failures, rather than fomenting hatred and resentment. All it takes is the pure and simple desire to come together as a community to commit constantly and tirelessly to the efforts of inclusion and integration, to help the fallen to their feet. At the same time, we might also sink down and feel condemned to repeat the mistakes of the violent, the blindly ambitious, those who spread mistrust and lies. Let others engage in the power plays of politics or economics. We should nurture that which is good and work in the service of goodness.

We could start from the bottom and fight for change on a concrete and local level—step by step, reaching to the distant corners of our world—with the same care and concern that the Good Samaritan showed for each of the wounded man's injuries. Let us seek out others and embrace the world as it is, without fear of pain or a sense of inadequacy, because in it lies all the goodness that God has sown in our hearts. Difficulties that might seem overwhelming are actually opportunities for growth and not excuses for sad inertia, which only leads to submission. Let us not undertake this on our own, individually.

DRY AWAY THE TEARS OF YOUR BRETHREN

"Comfort, comfort my people" are the heartfelt words of the prophet Isaiah that continue to make themselves heard today, bringing hope to all those who experience suffering and pain (Isa. 40:1). Let us never allow ourselves to be robbed of the hope that stems from our faith in the Risen Lord. True, we are often sorely tested, but we must never question the Lord's love for us. His mercy finds expression in the closeness, affection and support that many of our brothers and sisters can offer us in times of sadness and affliction. The drying away of tears is a concrete act that can break the cycle of solitude in which we often find ourselves trapped.

IF YOU EXPERIENCE THE DARKNESS OF SOLITUDE

Sisters and brothers, if you feel the darkness of solitude, if you feel as though a boulder obstructs your path to hope, if your heart has a festering wound, if you see no way out, then open your heart to the Holy Spirit. St. Bonaventure tells us that "where the trials are greater, He brings greater comfort, not like the world, which comforts and flatters us when things go well but derides and condemns us when they do not."* That is what the world does and, in particular, that is what the hostile spirit, the devil, does. First, he flatters us and makes us feel invincible—the flattery of the devil feeds our vanity—and then he flings us down and makes us feel like failures. He toys with us. He does everything to depress us, while the Spirit of the Risen Lord wants to elevate us. Look at the Apostles: they were alone that morning, alone and bewildered, cowering behind closed doors, living in fear, overwhelmed by their weaknesses, failings and sins because they had denied Christ. The years spent alongside Jesus had not changed them at all: they were no different than they had once been. Then they received the Spirit and everything changed: their problems and flaws remained but they were no longer afraid of them, just as they were no longer afraid of anyone who showed them hostility. They felt comforted within and wanted to share the abundant comfort of God. While before they were fearful, later their only fear was not to bear witness to the love they received.

WE NEED EVERYONE

We must rediscover the belief that we need one another, that we have a shared responsibility for other people and for the world, that being good and decent are worth it. We have tolerated moral degradation for too long; ethics, goodness, faith and

---

* *The Sunday Sermons of St. Bonaventure* (2008), https://muse.jhu.edu/book/14570; Sermon 22: Sunday in the Octave of Easter, pp. 269–277.

honesty have for too long been mocked. It is time to acknowledge that a light-hearted superficiality does us no good. The destruction of the foundations of social life sets one person against another in a battle over personal interests, gives rise to new forms of violence and brutality, and impedes the development of a true culture focused on caring for the environment.

St. Therese of Lisieux invites us to take the lesser road of love: to always offer a kind word, a smile or a small gesture that sows peace and friendship. An integrated ecology is comprised of small daily gestures that serve to break down the logic of violence, exploitation and selfishness. In a similar vein, the world of exaggerated consumption is a world that continually mistreats life in all its forms.

CAMARADERIE AND SOCIAL FRIENDSHIP

There is an episode in the life of St. Francis that shows the boundlessness of the saint's spirit and how he transcended differences of origin, nationality, skin color and religion. His journey to visit Sultan Malik al-Kamil in Egypt represented a considerable hardship for him, given his poverty, scarce resources, the great distance and the different language, culture and religion of the people he went to meet. This was also the era of the Crusades, and taking that journey is further proof of the breadth of his love and how he sought to embrace everyone. Francis' faithfulness to the Lord was matched only by his love for his brothers and sisters. Aware of the difficulties and dangers involved in the journey, Francis went to meet the Sultan with the same attitude that he asked of his disciples: if they were to find themselves "among the Saracens and other nonbelievers, they should not engage in arguments or disputes, but submit to others out of love for God" (1 Peter 2: 13–17). In that era, this was an extraordinary request. It is impressive how, eight hundred years ago, St. Francis urged his followers to avoid all forms of hostility and conflict and to show instead a humble and fraternal form of "submission," even with people who did not share his faith.

Francis did not wage a war of words aimed at imposing doctrines but communicated the love of God. He understood that "God is love. Whoever lives in love lives in God, and God in them" (1 John 4:16). In this way, he became a father to all, inspiring a vision of a fraternal society; for only a man who approaches others as they would have him approach, not to draw them into his own life but to help them become ever more fully themselves, can truly be called a father. The world in that era bristled with watchtowers and defensive walls; cities were the setting for brutal wars between powerful families, while poverty spread through the neglected outskirts. It was there that Francis experienced true peace, freed himself of the desire to wield power over others, joined the ranks of the poor and sought to live in harmony with all.

WHEREVER YOU ARE, MAKE PEACE!

We are called on to rekindle in our hearts an impulse of hope, which must be translated into concrete works of peace. You do not get along with someone? Make peace! Is there trouble at home? Make peace! Is there arguing in your community or at work? Make peace! Work for peace, reconciliation and fellowship. Each of us must perform gestures of fraternity towards our neighbor, especially those who are being tested by family tensions or other kinds of conflict. Small gestures such as these are of great value: they can be seeds of hope, forge paths and lead to peace.

A NEW ALLIANCE BETWEEN YOUNG AND OLD

We need a new covenant between young and old: we need to share the treasure of life, to dream together, to overcome generational conflicts and prepare the future for all. Without this alliance of life, dreams and future, we risk dying of hunger. At the same time, broken relationships, loneliness, selfishness and disintegration are on the rise.

We have often allowed societal life to be governed by the notion of "each man for himself." But this is deadly! Scripture would have us share what we are and what we possess, for only in this way will we find fulfillment. I have often referred to the words of the prophet Joel about young and old coming together (cf. Joel 2:16). Young people are prophets of the future and treasure their history; the elderly are tireless dreamers willing to share their experiences with the young, without standing in their way.

We need to embrace the young and old, the treasure of tradition and the freshness of the Spirit. Young and old together. In society and in the Church, together.

DIALOGUE AND IDENTITY

There can be no connection between nations without a love for one's own land, people, culture. I cannot truly encounter another unless I possess a foundation in which I stand firmly rooted, for it is on the basis of this that I accept the gift the other brings, offering in exchange an authentic gift of my own. I can only welcome others' differences and value their unique contributions if I feel connected to my own people and culture. Just as everyone loves and cares for his or her native land and village, they should also love and care for their home and assume the responsibility for its upkeep.

The truth is that a healthy and open perspective never constitutes a threat to one's identity. A living culture is always enriched by diversity because it never imports a mere copy of the new elements but integrates them into its society in a unique way. The result is a new synthesis that is ultimately beneficial to all; even the culture that gave rise to these contributions is, in turn, nourished.

WALLS TO AVOID

There is an excessively local kind of narcissism that does not communicate a healthy love for one's own people and culture. On the contrary, it conceals a closed spirit that stems from insecurity and fear of the other, and it chooses to erect defensive walls to protect itself. It is impossible to be local in a way that is healthy without being genuinely open to the universal, without being affected by what is happening in other parts of the world, without being enriched by other cultures, and without showing solidarity for the tragedies that befall other people. An excessively local narcissism instead focuses on a limited number of ideas, customs and certainties; it is incapable of admiring the vast potential and beauty that the greater world offers; it lacks an authentic and generous spirit of solidarity. Life at this local level no longer welcomes others, it is not interested in allowing the other to fill its gaps. Consequently, its possibilities for development are limited, it becomes static and falls ill. Healthy cultures, on the other hand, are naturally open and receptive.

LET US BUILD A CULTURE OF CARE

Peace can be built if we find peace within ourselves—inner peace, in our hearts—and with those who live beside us if we remove the obstacles that prevent us from caring for those in need, the indigent. To do so we need to develop a mentality and culture of "caring," a culture that fights the indifference, rejection and rivalry that unfortunately prevail today. We need to do away with these attitudes. Peace is not only the absence of war. Peace is never sterile, it does not exist in a *quirófano*, the Spanish word for operating theatre. Peace is part of life. Peace is not only the absence of war, it is a life that is rich in meaning, direction, experience, personal fulfillment and sharing. Only then does peace—so deeply longed for and always threatened by violence, selfishness and evil, always at risk—become possible. Peace is achievable only if we take it on as a task given to us by God.

But human strength alone is not enough, because peace is above all a gift, a gift of God. Peace should be implored with endless prayer, sustained with patient and respectful dialogue, and constructed openly and collaboratively, with the aid of truth and justice and through respecting the fair aspirations of individuals and people. My hope is that peace may reign in the hearts of men and women, in families, in places of work and recreation, in communities and in nations. In families, at work, in nations: may there be peace.

A MARVELOUS AND SHARED PILGRIMAGE

When our hearts are truly open to universal communion, nothing and no one is excluded from this sense of fellowship. It logically follows that any indifference or cruelty we show toward other creatures in this world will sooner or later affect how we treat other human beings. We have but one heart: the same wretchedness that leads us to mistreat an animal will soon be detected in our relationships with other people. Every act of cruelty toward any creature goes against human dignity. We can hardly consider ourselves to be loving if we disregard any aspect of reality. All is connected, human beings are united as brothers and sisters on a wonderful pilgrimage, bound together by God's love for each of His creatures, which also unites us with tenderness and affection to brother sun, sister moon, brother river and mother earth.

ELEVEN

AGAINST THE CURRENT

AGAINST "THROWAWAY CULTURE"

Feverish consumerism can overwhelm our hearts with superfluous objects. An obsession with entertainment and pleasure may seem like the only way to escape problems, when it really only delays them. A fixation on entitlement often leads us to neglect our responsibility for helping others. Then there is the great misunderstanding that surrounds love, which to many appears to be all about strong emotions, when actually loving is a gift, a choice and a sacrifice. These days, making a choice means not letting yourself be domesticated or homogenized, not letting yourself be anesthetized by a consumerism that erases originality, not giving into the cult of appearances. Making a choice today means fighting "throwaway culture" and the desire to have "everything immediately" and instead direct our lives toward the goal of heaven, toward God's dreams.

ARTIFICIAL LIGHT AND LIGHT OF PEACE

The light that the world offers us is artificial. It can be as bright as fireworks or like the flash of a camera. It might be stronger than the light of Jesus, which is gentle and quiet. The light of Jesus is like that of Christmas Eve: unpretentious, it offers and brings peace. The light of Jesus is not showy because it comes from the heart. It is true that the devil —and St. Paul often reminds us of this—frequently comes dressed as an angel of light. He likes to imitate the light of Jesus. He tries to seem good and speaks to us calmly, the same way he spoke to Jesus after fasting in the wilderness: "If you are the Son of God," he said, "throw yourself down." (Matthew 4:6) But he says it gently and deceptively.

This is why I urge you to ask the Lord for the wisdom to discern when it is Jesus who gives us light and when it is the devil who comes in the disguise of an angel. So many people believe they live in the light when they actually exist in the shadows— but they do not realize it! Let us therefore ask the Lord to give us the grace of His light and teach us to distinguish His light from the artificial one, created by our Enemy to deceive us.

WHAT ARE MY EYES REALLY SEEING?

How do I look at things? Do I look at things carefully, or do I glance at them the way I scroll rapidly through the thousands of photos on my phone or on social media? These days we often witness events first-hand without truly living them! Sometimes our initial reaction is to film them without even bothering to look into the eyes of the people involved.

All around us, and often even inside us, is death: it might be physical, spiritual, emotional or social. Do we really see it or do we just tolerate it? Can't we do anything to bring back life?

AGAINST THE SPINELESS

We do not want young people who are spineless, who are scared to fight or lukewarm about things. We do not want young people who get tired easily, who are always weary, with constantly bored looks on their faces. We want strong young people. We want young people full of hope and strength. Why? Because they know Jesus, they know God. Because their hearts are free. Liberating your heart, however, requires sacrifice, it means going against the current. The Beatitudes are Jesus' plan for us. They are a plan that goes against the current. Jesus says, "Blessed are those who are poor in spirit." He does not say, "Blessed are the rich, who make lots of money." No. The blessed are those who are poor in spirit, who are capable of approaching and understanding the poor. Jesus does not say, "Blessed are those who are having a ball," but rather, "Blessed are those who suffer the pain of others."

AGAINST THE ARROGANT

In the third Beatitude, Jesus says, "Blessed are the meek, for they will inherit the earth" (Matt. 5:5). Meekness, brothers and sisters! Meekness is one of the qualities of Jesus, who said of Himself, "Learn from me, for I am gentle and humble in heart" (Matt. 11:29). The meek are those who know how to control themselves and who leave room for others by listening to them, respecting their ways of life, needs and requests. They do not care about being stronger than or weakening others, they do not want to tower over and dominate everything, nor do they want to impose their ideas or their interests to the detriment of others. These people, who are scorned by those with a secular outlook, are precious in the eyes of God; He grants them the Promised Land, eternal life. This Beatitude begins here on earth and concludes in heaven, in Christ. Meekness. In this day and age, with all the fighting that exists, the first thing we release is aggression, defensiveness. We need meekness to move forward on the path of holiness. We need to listen, to respect and not to attack.

Dear brothers and sisters, choose purity, meekness and mercy. By entrusting yourself to the Lord, by being poor in spirit and suffering affliction, by dedicating yourself to justice and peace, you go against the current of the temporal world and its culture built on possession, mindless fun and arrogance against the weak.

FOR JUSTICE, AGAINST INJUSTICE

"Blessed are those who hunger and thirst for righteousness" is the Beatitude directed to those who fight for justice, so that there may be justice in the world (Matt. 5:6). Blessed are those who fight against injustice, Jesus tells us. This doctrine goes against the current of what the world tells us today.

AGAINST MATERIALISM

The Beatitudes of Jesus offer us a revolutionary model for happiness that goes against prevailing wisdom and what the media generally communicates. Secular thinking finds it shocking that God became one of us and died on a cross! According to temporal logic, the people whom Jesus proclaimed as blessed are often considered "losers" and worthless; instead, the qualities that usually get exalted are success, affluence, arrogance, power and self-justification at the expense of others.

A LIFE OF MODESTY

Wealth assures you of nothing at all. On the contrary, when the heart feels rich, we become so self-satisfied that there is no room for the Word of God, for loving our brothers and sisters, or for finding pleasure in the most important aspects of life. The heart is stripped of the greatest treasures of all. This is why Jesus says that blessed are those who are poor in spirit, those who have poverty in their hearts, for in those situations, the Lord can enter with His perennial newness.

This spiritual poverty is closely linked to what St. Ignatius of Loyola calls "holy indifference," which leads us to inner freedom. As he says, "It is necessary to make ourselves indifferent to all created things, as much as we are able, so that we do not necessarily want health rather than sickness, riches rather than poverty, honor rather than dishonor, a long rather than a short life, and so in all the rest."*

---

* *The First Principle and Foundation from the Spiritual Exercises [23] of Ignatius of Loyola*, A Literal Translation by Elder Mullan, SJ, and edited by Rick Rossi (2015).

Luke, meanwhile, does not speak of poverty "of spirit" but of those who are simply "poor" (cf. Luke 6:20). In so doing, he invites us to live a plain and austere life. He calls on us to share in the life of those most in need, the way the Apostles lived and, ultimately, to follow the example of Jesus who, although rich, "became poor" (2 Cor. 8:9).

To be poor at heart—this is holiness.

THROUGH SHARING, JESUS OFFERS US MIRACLES

Jesus does not create the loaves and fishes out of nothing. No. He works with what the disciples bring Him. One of them says, "Here is a boy with five small barley loaves and two fish, but how far will they go among so many?" (John 6:9). There is little, hardly anything at all, but it is enough for Jesus.

Let us now try and put ourselves in the shoes of that boy. The disciples ask him to share everything he has to eat. This seems unreasonable and even unfair. Why deprive a person, moreover a boy, of what he has brought from home and has the right to keep for himself? Why take away from one person what surely will not be enough to feed all? In human terms, it is illogical. But not for God. On the contrary, thanks to that small—and thus heroic—gift, Jesus feeds everyone. This is a great lesson for us. It tells us that the Lord can do a great deal with the little we put at His disposal. It would be so good if each day we asked ourselves, "What can I offer Jesus today?" He can do so much with just one of our prayers, with a charitable gesture toward others, even with one of our tribulations, if placed at His mercy. Let us give our smallness to Jesus and He will work miracles. God loves to do things like this: He builds great things from small, seemingly insignificant things. We like to add, we like addition; Jesus likes subtraction, taking something away so it can be given to others. We want to multiply things for ourselves; Jesus likes dividing up things and sharing them among others, He likes sharing. It is interesting that in the accounts of the multiplication of the loaves in the Bible, the verb "multiply" is never used. On the contrary, the verbs that are used all have the opposite meaning: "distributed," "broke," "divided," "gave" (cf. John 6:11; Matt. 14:19; Mark 6:41; Luke 9:16). But the verb "to multiply" is never used. The true miracle, Jesus tells us, is not multiplication, which produces vanity and power, but the division of things and sharing, which increases love and allows God to perform wonders. Let us try and share more. Let us try and do things the way Jesus teaches us.

Even today, the multiplication of goods does not solve problems if there is not an equitable sharing. The great tragedy of famine comes to mind, which affects children in particular. It has been officially calculated that every single day, around the world, approximately seven thousand children under the age of five die because of malnutrition, because they do not have what they need to survive. Faced with this scandal, the words of Jesus are like an invitation to us, not unlike the one the boy in the Gospel received, a boy with no name, who could be all of us. It is as if Jesus is saying to us, "Be brave, give what little you have, give of your gold and possessions, make them available to Jesus and your brothers and sisters. Do not be afraid, nothing will be lost, because if you divide, God will multiply. Banish the false modesty of feeling inadequate and trust in yourself. Believe in love, believe in the power of service, believe in the strength of gratuitousness."

LET THEM THINK THAT YOU ARE FOOLISH...

Jesus says no to war, no to hatred! Peace and compassion! Some people might object and say, "If I behave meekly, people will think I am a fool." This may be so, but let others think that. Be meek, because with meekness you shall inherit the earth!

GOD IS ALWAYS NEW

God is always new, He always urges us to set out anew, to change things up, to go beyond the familiar and into the fringes and margins. He leads us to a place where humanity is most wounded, where men and women, underneath all appearances, beneath superficiality and far from conformity, continue to seek the meaning of life. God is not afraid! He is fearless! He is always greater than all our plans, He is unafraid of the fringes. He Himself became a fringe (cf. Phil. 2:6–8; John 1:14). If we dare venture into the fringes, we will find Him there. He is already there. Jesus precedes us: He is in the hearts of our brothers and sisters, in their wounded flesh, in their oppressed lives and in their profound desolation. He is already there.

BE PROUD TO GO AGAINST THE CURRENT

What does it mean "to give up one's life for Jesus"? It can happen in two ways: by explicitly confessing one's faith or by implicitly defending the truth. Martyrs are the greatest example of how people gave up their lives for Christ. Over the course of two thousand years, an immense legion of men and women have sacrificed their lives in the name of Jesus Christ and the Word of God. And today, all around the world, a vast number of martyrs exist: they give up their lives for Christ and are put to death because they refuse to betray Jesus Christ. This is our Church. We have more martyrs today than we did in the early centuries! However, there is also daily martyrdom, which does not entail death but still represents a "giving up of life" for Christ by doing one's duty with love, according to the logic of Jesus, the logic of giving, making a sacrifice. Let us reflect on how many mothers and fathers turn to their faith by offering their own lives for the wellbeing of the family! Let us reflect on it! How many priests, brothers and sisters generously carry out their service for the kingdom of God! How many young people give up their own interests to dedicate themselves to children, the disabled, the elderly... They too are martyrs! Martyrs in everyday life!

And then there are people, both Christians and non-Christians, who "give up their lives" in the name of truth. Christ said, "I am the truth" and therefore whoever serves the truth serves Christ. One person who gave up his life for the truth is John the Baptist. John was chosen by God to prepare the way for Jesus: he was the one who told the people of Israel that Jesus was the Messiah, the Lamb of God who takes away the sin of the world (cf. John 1:29). John consecrated himself entirely to God and to His envoy, Jesus. But what happened in the end? He died in the name of truth when he denounced the adultery of King Herod and Herodias. How many people pay dearly for their commitment to truth! How many people prefer to go against the current rather than betray their conscience, the voice of truth! We must not be afraid! To the youth of today I say: Do not be afraid to go against the current. When they want to rob us of hope, when they offer us values that have spoiled like food gone bad, or values that harm us, we must go against the current! You, young people, go first: go against the current and do so with pride. Be proud to go against the current!

TWELVE

YOU HAVE EYES,
SO CONTEMPLATE

LET US BE IN SILENCE

Today, nature is no longer admired or contemplated but "devoured." We have become voracious, we rely on immediate profits and results, at all costs. We skim quickly over reality, always more distracted and superficial; we burn rapidly through news cycles and forests alike. We are sick with consumerism. This is our illness! We are sick with consumerism. We are eager to possess the latest app but we do not know the names of our neighbors, much less how to tell one tree from another. And, even worse, this lifestyle tears up our roots, we lose a sense of gratitude for what we have and for those who gave it to us. In order not to forget, we must return to contemplation; we must not be distracted by a thousand useless things, we must rediscover silence; for the heart not to fall ill, we must stay still. This is not easy. We need, for example, to free ourselves from the imprisonment of our mobile phones and look into the eyes of the people we are with. We need to look upon Creation, which was given to us.

Contemplation is the gift of time, so we can be in silence, pray, restore harmony to our souls, find a healthy balance between head, heart and hands, or between thought, feeling and action. Contemplation is the antidote to hasty, superficial and inconclusive choices. Those who contemplate learn to feel the ground under their feet and what support it offers; they learn that they are not alone and without meaning in the world. They discover the tenderness of God's gaze and understand how precious they are. Everyone is important to God, everyone can transform a part of the world that has been polluted by human voracity into the wonderful reality brought into being by the Creator. Those who know how to contemplate do not sit idly by but work to bring change. Contemplation leads to action.

WORDS OF LOVE SURROUND US

Nature is filled with words of affection, but how can we hear them when they are drowned out by constant noise, by interminable and nerve-wracking distractions, or by the cult of appearances? Many people today experience a profound imbalance that drives them to undertake frenetic activity which makes them feel busy; but this constant busy-ness leads them to damage everything around them. It even has an effect on how they treat the environment. Integrated ecology means taking the time to restore a serene sense of harmony with Creation; it means reflecting on our lifestyle and our ideals, and contemplating the Creator, who lives among us and in all things, whose presence must not be contrived but found, uncovered.

A manifestation of this is when we stop and give thanks to God before and after meals. I would ask all faithful to bring back this precious custom and live it with meaning. This moment of blessing, however brief, reminds us of our dependence on God for life, strengthens our feeling of gratitude for the gifts of Creation, acknowledges those who have labored so we have our goods and reaffirms our solidarity with those in greatest need.

ADULTS WITH YOUTHFUL HEARTS

I hope you young people respect yourselves enough, that you are serious enough about yourselves and that you will make all efforts to grow spiritually. This does not mean losing your sense of spontaneity, vivacity, enthusiasm or gentleness. Becoming older does not mean losing the best aspects of youth. Otherwise, the Lord could reproach you one day by saying, "I remember the devotion of your youth, how as a bride you loved me, and followed me through the wilderness" (Jer. 2:2).

GOODNESS GROWS IN HIDING

Sometimes the din of the world and the numerous activities that fill our days prevent us from slowing down and observing how the Lord is conducting history. And yet—the Bible assures us—God is always at work, like a good little seed that silently and slowly germinates. Little by little, it grows into a lush tree, giving life and providing shade and rest to everyone. The seeds of our good works might seem like small things, and yet all that is good pertains to God, and thus humbly and slowly bears fruit.

Let us always remember that goodness grows in a humble, hidden and often invisible way.

A WAY OF BEING HUMAN

Contemplation for human beings is a bit like the "salt" of life: it gives flavor, it seasons our days. Contemplation can happen when we gaze at the sunrise in the early morning, or admire how trees deck themselves out in green come spring; contemplation happens when we listen to music or to the sounds of the birds, when we read a book or admire a work of art or the masterpiece that is the human face... Carlo Maria Martini, who was asked to be bishop of Milan, entitled his first Pastoral Letter "The contemplative dimension of religious life." Effectively, people who live in large cities—where everything, it could be said, is artificial and functional above all—risk losing the ability to contemplate. Contemplation is less a way of doing than a way of being. Being contemplative does not depend on the eyes but on the heart.

CONTEMPLATING MEANS CARING

We need to be silent, we need to listen, we need to contemplate. Contemplation even heals the soul. Without contemplation, we become predators and forget our vocation as caretakers of life. It is key that we reacquire a contemplative dimension to life. We need to look at the earth and all of Creation as a gift, not like something to be exploited for profit. When we contemplate, we discover in others and in nature something vaster than only their usefulness. This is the heart of the issue: contemplating something means going beyond a utilitarian understanding of it. Contemplating that which is beautiful does not mean exploiting it: contemplation is free of charge. We discover the intrinsic value of things as they were granted by God.

Contemplation, which leads us to want to take care of things, does not mean looking at nature from the outside, as if we were not part of it. On the contrary, it is done from within, by recognizing ourselves as part of Creation, as key players and not mere spectators of an amorphous reality that exists only to be exploited. Those who contemplate in this manner experience wonder not only at what they see, they feel like they are an integral part of this beauty, and feel called upon to guard it and protect it. There is one thing we must not forget: people who do not know how to contemplate nature and Creation do not know how to contemplate people with all their inner riches. Those who live to exploit nature end up exploiting people and treating them like slaves. This is a universal law. If you do not know how to contemplate nature, it is unlikely you will know how to contemplate the inner beauty of people, your brothers and sisters.

Those who know how to contemplate, meanwhile, will be more inclined to work to change the things that produce degradation and that are harmful to our health. They will commit to educating and promoting new habits of production and consumption. They will contribute to a new model of economic growth that guarantees respect for our common home and for people. A contemplative person who takes action tends to become a guardian of the environment, which is wonderful! All of us should become guardians of the purity of the environment. We should try to combine the thousands of years of knowledge of our ancestors with new technological advancements, so that we may continue to live in a sustainable way.

LEARN FROM MARTHA AND MARY

Martha and Mary, sisters of Lazarus, lived in Bethany. They were faithful disciples of the Lord. Scripture describes them in this way: Mary sat at the feet of Jesus "listening to what he said," while Martha was "distracted by all the preparations that had to be made" (Luke 10:39–40). Both welcome the Lord on His brief visit but in a different way. Mary sits at His feet to listen while Martha busies herself to the extent that she even says to Jesus: "Lord, don't you care that my sister has left me to do the work by myself? Tell her to help me!" And Jesus replies by scolding her sweetly: "'Martha, Martha,' the Lord answered, 'you are worried and upset about many things, but few things are needed—or indeed only one'" (Luke 10:40–42).

What does Jesus mean by this? What is this one thing we need? First of all, it is important to understand that the story is not about two contradictory attitudes: listening to and contemplating the Word of the Lord as compared with offering practical assistance and service to our neighbor. These are not two opposing attitudes but two essential aspects of a Christian life, aspects that can never be separated but lived in profound unity and harmony. Why is Martha scolded, even if gently, by Jesus? Because she thought that what she was doing was the only important thing worth doing: she was too absorbed and worried about all the things that needed to be done. For a Christian, works of service and charity are never separate from the main source of our actions: listening to the Word of the Lord and sitting—like Mary—at the feet of Jesus, with a disciple's attitude. And this is why Martha was scolded.

May prayer and action always be closely united in our own Christian lives. Prayer that does not lead to a practical action that assists a brother or sister—be they poor, sick, in need of help or in difficulty—is a sterile and incomplete prayer. But, at the same time, when we focus in our ecclesial service only on doing, we give too much weight to things, functions and structures. We forget the centrality of Christ. We do not set aside time for dialogue with Him in prayer and we risk serving ourselves and not God, who is present in our needy brother and sister. St. Benedict summarized the lifestyle that he encouraged for his monks with these words: *ora et labora*, pray and work. The capacity to live and carry forth the love of God, to share His mercy and tenderness with others is born from contemplation, from a solid friendship with the Lord. The work we do with our needy brethren, our charitable works of mercy, also lead us to the Lord, because we see the Lord Himself in our needy brother and sister.

MEDITATION ALLOWS US TO STOP AND TAKE A BREATH

The practice of meditation has received a great deal of attention in recent years. It is not only Christians who talk about it: meditation is a fundamental part of almost all the world's religions. But it is also a widespread activity among people who do not have a religious perspective in life. We all need to meditate, reflect, rediscover ourselves: it is a dynamic human need. Especially in the voracious Western world, people seek meditation because it offers a barrier against the daily stresses of life and the sense of emptiness that surrounds us. And so we see images of both young people and adults sitting in recollection, in silence, with eyes half shut... We might ask ourselves, what are those people doing? They are meditating. It is a phenomenon to be looked on favorably. Indeed, we are not built for rushing madly about all the time; our inner lives should not be trampled. Everyone benefits from meditation. In some ways, meditating is like stopping to breathe.

AN ATTENTION THAT SHOULD NOT BE LOST

It is not healthy to love silence and yet avoid interaction with others, to seek out peace and quiet but avoid activity, to find time to pray but underestimate the value of service. Everything can be accepted and integrated into our lives and become a part of our path to holiness. We are called on to be contemplative even in the midst of action; we grow in holiness by responsibly and generously carrying out our mission.

PRAYER IS NOT A WALK IN THE PARK

Christian prayer, like all of Christian life, is not a walk in the park. None of the prayerful people we encounter in the Bible and in the history of the Church had an easy time with prayer. Yes, it is true, one can pray like a parrot, repeating words meaninglessly—blah, blah, blah—but that is not prayer. Prayer definitely brings great peace but always after an inner struggle that is sometimes arduous and often long. Prayer is not easy and that is why we often try to avoid it. Whenever we want to pray, so many other thoughts and activities come to mind, all of which seem more important and urgent. This even happens to me: I go to pray and then I start thinking about things I should be doing... We run away from prayer, I am not sure why, but we do. Then, after postponing our prayer time, we realize that those things we felt we had to do were not all that important. Actually, they may have been a waste of time. This is how the Enemy deceives us.

All godly men and women agree that prayer brings joy but that it can also be wearisome and annoying. Adhering to the how and when of prayers can be a struggle. Some saints pray for years without ever deriving joy from it, without perceiving its purpose. Silence, prayer and concentration are all difficult mental exercises, and yet sometimes human nature chooses to rebel. We would rather be anywhere else in the world but not there, in that church pew, praying. Those who want to pray need to remember that faith is not easy and that sometimes our faith advances in almost total darkness, without any points of reference. There are moments in the life of the faithful that are dark, which some saints call "the dark night" because we hear and see nothing.

And yet I continue to pray.

HE WHO PRAYS CARRIES THE WORLD

Those who pray never fully turn their backs on the world. If prayer does not tap into our joys and sorrows, our hopes and anxieties, it remains "ornamental," superficial, dramatic and solipsistic. We all need to care for our inner lives: to retreat into a space and time that is devoted to our relationship with God. But this does not mean avoiding reality. In prayer, God "takes us, blesses us, then breaks us and gives us" to all, satisfying the hunger of all. Every single Christian is called on to become bread in God's hands, to be broken and shared. In the same way, prayer needs to be real, not an escape.

This is why holy men and women seek solitude and silence. It is not because they do not want to be disturbed, but to better hear God's voice. Sometimes they retreat from the world altogether and withdraw into their own rooms, as Jesus recommended (cf. Matt. 6:6). Wherever they are, however, the doors to their hearts are wide open to those who pray without actually knowing how, to those who do not pray but carry a muffled cry of pain within like a hidden invocation, and to those who have erred and lost the way... Anyone can knock on the door of a prayerful person and they will find a compassionate and open heart. Prayer is both our beating heart and our voice; it gives a heart and voice to people who do not know how to pray, who do not want to pray or for whom it is impossible to pray: we are the intermediaries so that their hearts and voices can rise up to Jesus, to the Father. Whether our solitude lasts a long time or just half an hour, those who pray step away from everything and everyone and discover everything and everyone in God. Prayerful people pray for the entire world, hoisting its sorrows and sins on their shoulders. They pray for each and every being, as if they were God's "antennae" in this world.

ST. ANTHONY'S STRUGGLE

St. Anthony the Abbot, the founder of Christian monasticism in Egypt, faced moments of great hardship, and prayer became a difficult struggle for him. His hagiographer, St. Athanasius, Bishop of Alexandria, writes that one of the worst episodes in the life of the hermit occurred when he was about thirty-five, which was middle-aged at that time, an age when many people go through periods of crisis. Anthony was disturbed by the ordeal but fought back. When he went back to his state of calm, he turned to his Lord with an almost reproachful tone. "Where wert thou? Why didst thou not appear at the beginning to make my pains cease?" Jesus replied, "Anthony, I was here. But I waited to see you fight."[*] Fighting through prayer. Indeed, prayer is very often a form of combat.

WITH PRAYER WE MAKE SPACE

We return to the same subject: prayer! Prayer is vastly important. We need to pray not only with the prayers we learned as children, but with our own words. We need to know how to ask the Lord, "Lord, help me, tell me what to do. What should I do now?" And through prayer we make room, so that the Spirit may come to us and help us, tell us what to do. Prayer is so important! Never forget to say your prayers. Never! You can pray on the bus or while walking down the street; no one can tell because we pray in the silence of our heart. Take advantage of those moments to pray; pray that the Spirit will tell you what to do.

---

[*] Athanasius Life of Anthony, 10, http://earlychurchtexts.com/public/athanasius_on_antony.htm.

LEARN TO KNOW WHAT TO SAY TO THE LORD

Jesus teaches us that the Father knows all. Do not worry, for the Father will send rain on good and sinners alike, and sunshine on good and sinners alike. How I wish that, from this day forward, each of us would pick up the Bible every day and for five minutes slowly recite Psalm 103: "Praise the Lord, my soul, and forget not all his benefits who forgives all your sins and heals all your diseases, who redeems your life from the pit and crowns you with love and compassion" (Ps. 103:2–4). Let us all recite it all. And in this way we will learn how to speak to the Lord, when we need to ask Him for grace.

WE ASK FOR GRACE BY FIGHTING FOR IT

Allow me to recount something I experienced first-hand when I was in Argentina. A married couple had a nine-year-old daughter who had an illness that the doctors were unable to diagnose. When the end was near, the doctor in the hospital said to the mother of the child, "Signora, it is time to call your husband." Her husband was at work; they were laborers. The doctor told the father, "The child will not make it through the night. She has an infection, there is nothing we can do." Although that man might not have gone to Mass each and every Sunday, he still had deep faith. He left in tears. He left his wife there with the little girl in the hospital and took the train to the Basilica of Our Lady of Luján, Patron of Argentina, seventy kilometers away. The Basilica was already closed as it was almost ten o'clock at night, but the man held on to the railing that surrounded the Basilica and prayed all night to Our Lady, fighting for his daughter's health. I am not inventing this: I myself saw him! I lived through it. I saw how that man fought. At six o'clock the next morning, the church doors opened and he walked in to pay his respects to Our Lady. After spending that whole night "fighting," he then went home. When he arrived home, no one was there, so he thought to himself, "My daughter is no longer with us. But no, Our Lady would never do that to me." Then he saw his wife and she smiled and said, "I do not know how it happened but the doctors said that something changed and now she is cured." That man, by fighting for his daughter with prayer, received the grace of Our Lady. Our Lady listened to him. I saw it: prayers can work miracles, because prayers go directly to the tenderness of God, who loves us like a father. And if He does not grant us a certain grace, He will grant us a different one at a different time. But to ask for grace, we must fight for it with prayer. Sometimes we ask for a grace that we need, but we ask weakly, without truly wanting it, without fighting for it. Serious things need to be fought for seriously. Prayer is a form of combat and the Lord is always with us.

If, in a moment of temporary blindness, we do not see His presence, we will see Him in the future. One day we, too, will say the same words that the patriarch Jacob said: "Surely the Lord is in this place, and I was not aware of it" (Gen. 28:16).

NOT ECSTASY, BUT PERSEVERANCE

We must continuously learn how to walk. True progress in spiritual life does not mean the multiplication of ecstasies; it means persevering in times of difficulty, to keep on walking, step after step. If you get tired, stop a bit and then start walking again. But keep walking with perseverance. Let us remember the parable by St. Francis about perfect joy: a friar's skill is not measured by the infinite fortunes that rain down from heaven but in how he continues on his path, even if he does not receive acknowledgment or if he is mistreated or if everything loses its initial flavor. All the saints passed through such "dark valleys." We should not be shocked to read their diaries and discover that they also went through difficult times, that sometimes they faced prayer listlessly, without enthusiasm. We must learn to say, "Even though You, my God, seem to be doing everything to make me stop believing in You, I will still continue to pray to You." Believers never just switch it off! Of course, their prayers may, at times, resemble the prayers of Job, who refused to accept that God treated him unjustly and protested and called Him to judgment. But, as an elderly lady I once knew said, "Even getting angry with God is a kind of prayer." Children often get angry with their fathers... It is a way of relating to God. We get angry at Him because we see Him as a father. And even we, who are far less holy and patient than Job, know that in the end—at the end of the period of hardship during which we have frequently raised our voices in silence to heaven and asked "Why?"—God will reply.

WE MIGHT ONLY BE A BREATH, BUT WE KNOW HOW TO PRAY

Humanity—men and women, all of us—are but a breath, a blade of grass. As the philosopher Pascal once wrote, "There is no need for the whole universe to take up arms to crush man: a vapour, a drop of water is enough to kill him." We are fragile beings but we know how to pray: this is our greatest dignity. It is also our strength.

THE MOTHER OF ALL PARABLES

There are many ways of receiving the Word of God. As we read in the parable of the sower, we can receive the Word as if we were a path, with birds swooping down to eat the seeds (cf. Matt. 13:1–23). The path represents distraction: a great danger of our time. Beset by endless small talk, ideologies and distractions both from the inside and outside, we can lose the pleasure of silence, reflection and dialogue with the Lord, to the degree that we also risk losing our faith and not hearing the Word of God. We try to see everything but everything distracts us.

Alternatively, we can receive the Word of God like the seeds that fall on a rocky patch of ground, with little soil. There seeds sprout quickly but they also wilt quickly because they cannot sink their roots down far. This image captures those who receive the Word of God with bright but brief enthusiasm, one that is superficial, without truly assimilating it. And then, at the first sign of trouble or hardship, some kind of displeasure or disturbance, that still-feeble faith dissolves, like a seed that lands among the rocks.

A third possibility that Jesus mentions in the parable sees us receiving the Word of God like a patch of ground where thorns grow. The thorns represent the deceit of wealth, success and secular concerns... There, the Word grows a bit but then is suffocated; it is not strong and it dies, it does not bear fruit.

Lastly—the fourth possibility mentioned in the parable—is that we may receive the Word as if we were good soil. Here, and here alone, does the seed take root and bear fruit. The seed falling on the fertile soil represents those who hear the Word, who embrace it, keep it safe in their hearts and put it into practice in everyday life.

This parable of the sower is something of the "mother" of all parables because it addresses how we listen to the Word of God. It reminds us that the Word is a seed that is fruitful and effective, God scatters it generously and everywhere, without being frugal. This is the heart of God! Each one of us is a patch of ground onto which the seed of the Word falls; no one is excluded! The Word is given to each of us. We can ask ourselves: what type of terrain am I? Do I resemble the path, the rocky ground or the thorny brambles? If we so choose, with the grace of God, we can become good soil, plowed and carefully cultivated, where the seed of the Word of God can grow to maturity.

TODAY IS THE MOST BEAUTIFUL DAY

There is no day more wonderful than the one we are living today. Some people live with the thought that "things will get better in the future," without taking each day as it comes. These people live in a dream, they do not know how to deal with concrete reality. Today is real, today is concrete. Prayer takes place today. Jesus comes toward us today, the day we are currently living. And prayer transforms today into a grace, or rather, it transforms us: prayer soothes anger, sustains love, multiplies joy, instills us with the strength to forgive. Sometimes it seems like it is not even us anymore who are living but that grace itself is living and working inside of us through prayer. And when we have an angry or unhappy thought, one that pushes us toward bitterness, let us stop and say to the Lord, "Where are you? And where am I going?" And the Lord will be there. The Lord will give us the right word, the right advice to move forward without the bitter taste of negativity. For prayer is always—to use a profane word—positive. Always. It will carry you forward. Each day that begins, if welcomed in prayer, is accompanied by courage, so that the problems we have to face no longer seem obstacles in the way of our happiness, but messages from God, chances to encounter Him. When a person is accompanied by the Lord, he or she feels more courageous, freer and happier.

THIRTEEN

DO NOT STOP DREAMING

BETTER OFF DON QUIXOTE THAN SANCHO PANZA

Jesus believes in you more than you believe in yourselves. Remember this because it is important: Jesus believes in you more than you believe in yourselves. Jesus loves you more than you love yourselves. Look for Him by stepping outside yourselves, on your path: He awaits you. Spend time with others, make friends, take walks, meet up: let this be going to Church, let this be your path. The Bible is the school of life, the Bible always leads us to our path. I believe that this is the way to prepare ourselves to hear the Lord.

Eventually you will hear the invitation by the Lord to do one thing or another... In the Bible, God says to some, "Follow me!" To others, He says, "Now do this..." The Lord will let you know what He wants from you, with the only condition being that you do not sit still, that you follow your path, that you look for others and interact with them, build a community and, most of all, pray. Use your own words to pray, use what comes from your heart. This is the most beautiful prayer that exists. Jesus always invites us to keep moving: do not stop when you reach the beach and see the horizon. Keep going. He does not want you sitting on the bench, He wants you on the playing field. He does not want you behind the scenes, or spying on others, or in the bleachers commenting on the game. He wants you front and center. Get out there and play! Are you worried about embarrassing yourself? Don't worry and just do it. We have all embarrassed ourselves before, a number of times. Losing face is not the worst thing that can happen in life. One of the worst things that can happen is that you do not put yourself out there: that is truly terrible! That is not making the most of your life! It is better to be carried away with beautiful dreams and embarrass yourself periodically than lead the quiet life of a pensioner: pot-bellied and comfy. Better to be a good idealist than a lazy realist: better off Don Quixote than Sancho Panza!

WE ARE NOT CHOSEN FOR SMALL THINGS

No difficulties, trials or misunderstandings should be feared as long as we remain tied to God like branches to a vine, as long as we take care of our friendship with Him, as long as we continue to make room for Him in our lives. This is especially true if we feel poor, weak and sinful, because God grants riches to our poverty, strength to our weakness, conversion and forgiveness to our sinfulness.

Let us trust in God's actions! With Him we can accomplish great things. He will grant us the joy of being His disciples and witnesses. Take a risk on great ideals, on important things. We Christians were not chosen by the Lord for little things. Always move forward, towards great things. Stake your lives on noble ideals!

RENEW YOUR FIRE AT ALL AGES

While young people are naturally attracted by the endless horizon that opens up before them, adults, with their interest in security and comfort, tend to gradually neglect that horizon and risk losing the exuberance of youth. In actual fact, the very opposite should happen: we should mature and continue to build our lives without losing that enthusiasm and openness to an ever-greater reality. At every phase in our lives, we can renew and increase our youthfulness. When I began my ministry as pope, the Lord broadened my horizons and granted me renewed youth. The same thing can happen to a couple who have been married for many years or to a monk in his monastery. Some things need time to settle but maturity can coexist with the rekindling of an inner fire, with a heart that is eternally young.

Growing older means preserving and nurturing the most precious aspects of our youth but it also involves being willing to clear away things that are not good, as well as receiving new gifts from God, who calls on you to develop the things that really matter. Sometimes, an inferiority complex might deter you from acknowledging your flaws and weaknesses. In so doing you might be blocking your growth and maturity. Instead, let yourself be loved by God for He loves you just as you are. He values and respects you, while continuing to offer you more: more of His friendship, more fervor in prayer, more hunger for His Word, more longing to receive Christ through the Eucharist, more desire to live by the Bible, more inner strength, more peace and spiritual joy.

IF THE ELDERLY DO NOT DREAM...

The dreams of the elderly, who have been shaped by experience and their years, are woven through with memories and images. If young people sink their roots into these dreams, they can peer into the future; they can have visions that will broaden their horizons and reveal new paths. But if the elderly do not dream, young people will lose sight of the horizon.

THERE'S NO FAITH WITHOUT RISK

In the parable of the talents, the best servants are those who *take a risk*. They are not fearful and overcautious, they do not cling to what they possess, they put their gold to good use. For if goodness is not invested, it is lost. The greatness of our lives is not measured by how much we save, but by the fruit we bear. So many people spend their lives simply accumulating wealth and possessions, concerned only with *living well* and not with *doing good*. But a life that is centered on *our own needs* and that is blind to *the needy* is empty! If we *have a gift* it is so that we can *be a gift* to others. And here, brothers and sisters, we should ask ourselves: Do I only follow my needs, or do I think of the needy? Do I extend a hand or close it in a fist?

It is important to note how the servants who invest their talents, who take a risk, are called "faithful" four times over (Matt. 25:21, 23). For the Gospel, faithfulness is never risk-free. "But Father, does being a Christian mean taking risks?" you ask. "Yes, dear ones, you must take risks. If you do not, you will end up like the third servant: you will bury your abilities, your spirituality and your material riches, everything." Take risks: there is no such thing as risk-free faith. Being faithful to God means handing over our life, letting our best-laid plans be disrupted by our need to serve. "I have plans but if I have to serve..." we say to ourselves. Let your plans be upset. Go and serve. It is sad to see Christians play defense only, content only to observe rules and obey commandments. Those "moderate" Christians never push the boundaries because they are afraid of taking risks. And—if you will permit me—those who choose to take care of themselves and avoid all risks start a process of mummification of their souls and end up as mummies. It is not enough to merely follow the rules: faith in Jesus is much more than not making mistakes. This is very wrong. But that is what the lazy servant in the parable of the talents thought: lacking in initiative and creativity, he hides behind empty fears and buries the gold he received. The master calls him "wicked" (Matt. 25:26). And yet he did nothing wrong! While this is true, he also did nothing good either. He preferred to sin by omission rather than risk making a mistake. He was not faithful to God, who gives generously of Himself. He offended Him in the worst way possible by returning the gift he had received: "You gave me this and I give it back." Nothing more.

DO NOT LET LIFE PASS YOU BY

The time to receive redemption is brief for all of us: it is as long as life. It is brief. It might seem long sometimes...I remember once going to administer the Holy Sacrament and the Extreme Unction to an elderly man who was full of goodness. Just before receiving the Eucharist and the Unction, he looked at me and said, "Life flew by." It was as if he were saying that he thought life would be eternal but instead, it just flew by. This is how we, the elderly, feel. Life flies by. Life is a gift of God's infinite love but also a time to prove our love for Him. This is why every moment, every instant of our existence is a precious opportunity to love God and our neighbor, and thereby enter into eternal life.

The histories of our lives have two separate rhythms: one is measurable in hours, days and years; the other is composed of the seasons of our development: birth, childhood, adolescence, maturity, old age and death. Each of these periods, each phase, has its own value, each offers a privileged occasion to encounter the Lord. Faith helps us discover the spiritual significance of these periods: each one contains a particular calling from the Lord to which we can give either a positive or negative response.

THE IMPORTANCE OF AWE

Let us start over with a sense of awe. Let us gaze upon Jesus on the cross and say to Him, "Lord, how much you love me! How precious I am to you!" Let us be awed by Jesus so that we can start living again, because the greatness of life lies not in possessions and promotions but in realizing that we are loved. This is the greatness of life: discovering that we are loved. And the greatness of life lies in the beauty of love. In crucified Jesus, we see God humiliated, the Almighty has been discarded. And with the grace of awe we realize that by embracing those who have been discarded, in assisting those who have been humiliated by life, we are loving Jesus. For He is among the last, He is in those who have been rejected, in those who our self-righteous culture condemns.

Immediately following the death of Jesus, the Gospel reveals the most beautiful representative of awe, the centurion. Upon seeing Jesus die, the centurion says, "Surely this man was the son of God!" (Mark 15:39). The man was awed by love. What did he see when Jesus died? He saw Jesus die with love and in love, and this brought him awe. Jesus suffered enormously but He never stopped loving. This is the awesomeness of God: He can even fill death with love. In that gratuitous and unprecedented love, the pagan centurion found God. *Surely this man was the son of God!* His words seal the Passion. We read in the Gospels that many before him admired Jesus for His miracles and for His prodigious works; many had acknowledged that He was the Son of God. But Christ had always silenced them, because He did not want people to think only in secular terms, that God was to be adored and feared for His power and might. Now Christ can no longer silence anyone. At the foot of the cross there can be no mistake: God revealed Himself and reigns with the unarmed and disarming power of love alone.

Brothers and sisters, God awes our minds and hearts. Let us be filled with that awe as we gaze upon the crucified Lord. May we be able to say: "You truly are the Son of God. You are my God."

WHEN ANXIETY AND INSECURITY MAKE INROADS

Keep following your hopes and dreams. But be careful. There is one temptation that can cause many problems: anxiety. Anxiety can be a hefty enemy; it can lead us to give up when we do not see instant results. Our most beautiful dreams are attained through hope, patience and commitment, and never in haste. At the same time, we should never hold back out of insecurity, we should never be afraid to take chances or make mistakes. On the contrary, we should fear paralysis, we should be afraid of becoming like the living dead, who do not really live because they are afraid of taking risks and carrying through on commitments, or because they are afraid of making mistakes. Even if you make a mistake and fall, you can always get back up and start over; no one has the right to rob you of hope.

WHERE JOY IS BORN

"My soul magnifies the Lord" (Luke 1:46). Perhaps we are accustomed to hearing these words, perhaps we no longer pay attention to their true meaning. To "magnify" literally means "to make great," to enlarge. Mary "aggrandizes the Lord" and not her own problems, which she certainly did not lack. How often we let ourselves be overwhelmed by our difficulties and absorbed by our fears! Our Lady does not; she puts God as the first greatness of life. From this springs the Magnificat, this is where joy is born. It is not born from the absence of problems, which we all have to face sooner or later, but from the presence of God who helps us, who is near us. Because

God is great. And, above all, God looks on the lowly ones. We are His weakness of love: God looks on and loves the lowly.

LET US REDISCOVER THE SENSE OF EXPECTATION

When a person thinks only of the present, he or she loses all sense of anticipation and expectation, which are beautiful and necessary, and which lead us away from the passing troubles of the moment. This attitude—when one loses the sense of expectation—precludes a view of the hereafter: we do everything as if we will never have to leave for the hereafter. And so we end up caring only about possessions, standing out, establishing ourselves... And more. If we let ourselves be led by what seems most attractive to us, by what we like, by following our interests, life becomes sterile; if we do not save up any oil for our lamp, it will go out before we can encounter the Lord. Yes, we must live today but our today must lean into tomorrow, towards that future encounter. Our present must be full of hope.

BEFORE ALL ELSE, DREAM!

A Latino writer once said that one of our eyes is made of flesh and the other of glass. With the eye of flesh we see what is in front of us. With the eye of glass we see our dreams. This is beautiful, is it not?

In the daily reality of life, there has to be room for dreaming. A young person who cannot dream is cut off, isolated. Everyone dreams of things that will never happen. But dream them anyway! Desire them, seek new horizons, be open to great things. In Argentina we say, "*No te arrugues*," which is like saying don't hold back, open up. Open up and dream! Dream that you can make a change in the world. Dream that if you give your best, you can help make this world a different place. Dream! At times you might get carried away and dream too much—but life will remind you of what is impossible. It does not matter; continue to dream. And share your dreams. Talk about the great things you desire, because the bigger you dream, the farther you will have traveled down your path, even if it gets cut short. So, first and foremost, dream!

FOURTEEN

HOW TO UNVEIL THE MARVEL THAT ABIDES IN YOU

MAKE DEFINITIVE AND RADICAL CHOICES

In our Christian lives, we have the choice of entrusting ourselves to the loyalty of the Lord. It is a great and difficult decision to make. We realize just how difficult a decision is when we learn about the lives of the martyrs, or when we read in the news about the persecution of Christians today. Let us reflect on our brothers and sisters who find themselves in extreme situations and who make this brave choice. They live in our day and age, and are an example to us.

FILL EACH MOMENT WITH LOVE

As you work to achieve your dreams, make the most of each day and do your best to fill each moment with love. Because it is true: today may be your last, so make the effort to live it as enthusiastically and deeply as possible.

DO NOT BE SHOCKED IF JESUS WALKS BY

"You are one of us," we could say to Jesus—and what a beautiful prayer that would be! Because He is one of us, He understands us, stands by us, forgives us and loves us deeply. Of course, it would be easier to believe in a more abstract and remote god, a god that does not get involved in complex situations and who accepts a faith that is distinct from life, problems and society. Or in a god with "special powers," one who makes exceptional things happen, always accompanied by strong emotions. Instead, brothers and sisters, God is incarnate: God is humble, God is kind, God stays hidden, He approaches us through the everyday. We may well make the same mistake that Jesus' fellow villagers did: not recognizing Him when He passes. Let me repeat the beautiful words of St. Augustine: "I fear the Lord God when He passes." But why are you afraid, Augustine? "I am afraid of not recognizing Him. I am afraid that the Lord will walk by: *Timeo Dominum transeuntem*." We do not see Him, we are shocked by Him. Let us reflect on this reality in our hearts.

DO NOT BE AFRAID OF GOD

When faced with the call from the Lord, which can reach us in a thousand ways, either through people, or through sad or happy events, our response may initially be one of rejection. We might reject Him because His call seems to go against our aspirations. Or else we might be afraid, because the call is too demanding and troublesome: "I could never do that, better not, I am better off living a quiet life... with God on that side, me on the other." But God's call is love, we need to perceive the love that exists behind each call and we should reply with love. This is the language we should use: the response to a call that comes from love can only be love. At the beginning there is an encounter, or rather, there is *the* encounter with Jesus, who tells us about the heavenly Father: He lets us experience His love. This leads to a desire to communicate it to the people we love: "I have discovered Love," "I have discovered the Messiah," "I have encountered God," "I have encountered Jesus," "I found the meaning of my life" we want to say. In a few words: "I have found God."

TAKE RISKS BUT KEEP MOVING FORWARD!

I frequently say, Take a risk! Those who do not take risks do not move forward on their path. "But what if I make a mistake?" Blessed be the Lord! You will make more mistakes if you sit still: that is a real mistake, a very bad mistake, that is closing yourself up. Take risks. Stake your claim on noble ideals, you might get your hands dirty, but take a chance the way the Good Samaritan did in the parable. When we live a relatively easy life, there is always the temptation of paralysis, the temptation to not take risks, to live a comfy and quiet life... Face the problem, step outside your comfort zone and take a risk. Otherwise you will slowly become paralyzed: happy, content, surrounded by family, comfortably parked. It is very sad to see people parked like cars; it is very sad to see people who seem more like mummies than living beings. Take risks! And if you make a mistake, blessed be the Lord. Take a risk!

ALWAYS FIND THE COURAGE TO GET TO YOUR FEET

Once a young woman said to me, "Some of my friends have lost all their enthusiasm, they do not want to get to their feet and move forward." Unfortunately, depression is spreading among young people, occasionally even leading them toward the temptation to take their own lives. Apathy reigns in so many situations, and people sink into an abyss of anguish and remorse! How many young people cry out with no one to hear their plea! Instead, they are met by looks of distraction and indifference from people concerned only with enjoying their "happy hour," people who always keep their distance.

MAKE NOISE WITH BEAUTY, GOODNESS AND TRUTH

I would like to say this: find courage, move forward and make some noise. Go on, do it! There will always be people in life who want you to slow down, who block your path. Please, go against the current. Be courageous and go against the current of our civilization, which is causing itself so much harm. Do you understand? Go against the current—and make some noise!—but do it while embracing the values of beauty, goodness and truth.

STRUCTURE YOUR JUBILANT NOISE

The other day, a priest jokingly said to me, "You keep telling young people to make noise, Holy Father, but we are the ones who have to deal with all the noise they make!" It is good to make noise, but help others by structuring your noise well. Organize your noise! The sound that comes from a heart that is free, the sound that comes from solidarity, the sound that brings us hope, the sound that comes when we find Jesus and God—this sound is our fortress. This is the kind of sound that I invite you to make.

STOP BEING NOSTALGIC FOR SLAVERY

On our journey of life there is the tendency to resist freedom; we are afraid of freedom and, paradoxically and often unwittingly, we prefer to be enslaved. Freedom scares us because it forces us to face up to time and our responsibility to live it well. Instead, slavery reduces time to a "moment" and we feel safer; under slavery, time is disconnected from its past and from its future. In other words, slavery prevents us from truly and fully living in the present because it empties time of the past and shuts the door on the future, on eternity. Slavery would have us believe that we cannot dream, fly or hope.

Once, a great Italian artist said that it was easier for the Lord to take the Israelites out of Egypt than to take Egypt out of the heart of the Israelites. They had been *physically* freed from slavery but, during their wandering in the desert, with all the difficulties and the hunger they faced, they began to feel nostalgic for Egypt: they recalled the "onions and garlic" they ate at no cost (cf. Num. 11:5). They forgot, however, that they ate these things at the table of slavery.

LIVE YOUR BEST LIFE!

Do not watch life go by from a balcony.

Do not confuse happiness with a comfortable sofa and do not live your lives behind a screen.

Do not let yourselves go like sad and abandoned vehicles!

Do not be parked cars; let your dreams blossom and make strong decisions.

Take risks, even if they turn out to be mistakes.

Do not go through life anesthetized and do not look at the world like tourists.

Make some noise!

Crush the fears that paralyze you so that you do not become mummies.

Live!

Live your best lives!

Open the cage doors and fly away!

And please, do not retire before your time.